the *Passion Driven* sermon

the Passion Driven sermon

Changing the Way Pastors Preach and Congregations Listen

Jim Shaddix

BROADMAN
&HOLMAN
PUBLISHERS

Nashville, Tennessee

0–8054–2722–8

Published by Broadman & Holman Publishers
Nashville, Tennessee

Dewey Decimal Classification: 251

Subject Heading: PREACHING \ PASTORAL THEOLOGY \
SERMONS—PHILOSOPHY

1 2 3 4 5 7 8 9 10 08 07 06 05 04 03

To
the faith communities of
Edgewater Baptist Church
and

New Orleans Baptist Theological Seminary
who graciously listen to me preach every week
for the glory of God

Contents

Foreword

In *Preaching and Preachers,* Martyn Lloyd-Jones made a distinction between pulpiteers and preachers. He described late nineteenth-century America as a culture where pulpiteers dominated—epitomized in Lloyd-Jones's assessment by Henry Ward Beecher. Lloyd-Jones wrote,

> These men were pulpiteers rather than preachers. I mean that they were men who could occupy a pulpit and dominate it, and dominate the people. They were professionals. There was a good deal of the element of showmanship in them, and they were experts in handling congregations and playing on their emotions. In the end they could do almost what they liked with them.[1]

Lloyd-Jones then solemnly added this: "These pulpiteers were to me—with my view of preaching—an abomination."

Lloyd-Jones's famous lectures on preaching, from which his book was drawn, represented a watershed of sorts. He was sounding a much-needed warning about the decline of *biblical* preaching. He was seeing the very beginning of a trend where entertainment, oratory, people-centered messages, and other pragmatic considerations were crowding out passionate biblical preaching.

Unfortunately, Lloyd-Jones's warning went largely unheeded—or was flatly rejected—by the mainstream of the evangelical movement. As a result, the art of pulpiteering is currently enjoying a renaissance that Lloyd-Jones could not have foreseen in his worst nightmares.

The trend is evident in the kind of books pastors are reading. Up to and including Lloyd-Jones's book, the most widely read books about preaching tended to focus on themes like the glory of God, biblical content, the Holy Spirit's empowerment, and the importance of preaching with courage and conviction. In the three decades since, the most popular books on preaching tend to be those preoccupied with meeting people's "felt needs," being "relevant," being "practical," being "user-friendly," being "contemporary," or otherwise adapting the message to fit the hearers' preferences. In other words, modern preaching is self-consciously shaped to fit a pragmatic agenda ("purpose-driven"), rather than being compelled and tempered by a passion for faithfully and courageously delivering the whole counsel of God.

In contrast to all that, Jim Shaddix gives us a *biblical* perspective of preaching. His analysis of the state of the modern pulpit is sharply focused and filled with insight. He has correctly diagnosed the problem, and he offers the right remedy. Plus, he writes with clarity, precision, and grace. I found myself giving a hearty amen to virtually every paragraph.

This book is a challenge to pulpiteers and an encouragement to preachers whose passion is for the truth of God's Word and the advancement of God's glory. I'm thrilled to see it in print and pray that it will be read by many.

John MacArthur

Acknowledgments

As always, I am deeply indebted to my wife—Debra—and my three wonderful children—Clint, Shane, and Dallys—for the love they give this husband, dad, pastor, and professor. Their patience and support make it possible for me to keep all the balls in the air.

Thanks to my president, Dr. Chuck Kelley, who has given me a platform from which to speak about pastoral preaching and an arena in which to practice it. The encouragement and opportunities he continues to offer make it possible for me to fulfill my dreams. I still pinch myself in the morning to see if it's real. As my preaching professor, Dr. Al Fasol, used to say, "I can't believe they pay me to do this!"

Thanks also to the Emmaus Road Group—Bradley, David, Tony, Landon, Byron B., Byron T., D. J., and Matt—for reviewing the manuscript and offering incredibly helpful advice. They provided invaluable insight from the hearts and minds of young pastors and preachers who proclaim God's Word in contemporary culture. And thanks to my colleague, Dr. Chuck Quarles, whose knowledge of the Greek New Testament helped me not to stray too far from the integrity of the 1 Corinthians text.

Many others have trod this path before me with greater diligence and detail. Their discoveries have made possible any meager contribution that I offer. I am especially indebted to John Piper, author of *The Supremacy of God in Preaching;* James W. Thompson, author of *Preaching Like Paul;* and John MacArthur Jr., none of whom I know personally. (But it would have been impossible for me to cite with precision and completeness the degree to which their books, tapes, and sermons have been meshed into my heart and mind over the years.) The values these men hold with regard to God's Word and the preaching event profoundly inspired, affirmed, and expanded my own ideas as I wrote. I can only hope that my journey might inspire others to allow their preaching to be driven by a passion for the glory of God!

Introduction

I have some questions.

The Questions Everybody Is Asking

"The problem with modern preaching is that we are not answering the questions people are asking." That was the stern rebuke of the closing speaker at an international preaching conference I was attending several years ago at the historic Westminster Chapel in London, England. The meeting featured some of the greatest preachers and teachers of God's Word from all over the globe. The subject under consideration was characteristic of the bywords and trends in preaching in the United States. We were talking about *relevance* in preaching. How do we preach to contemporary culture so that we are sure to connect? It was—and still is—a worthy subject indeed. During the closing session, we were addressed by a popular Baptist minister from England who was both intriguing and inspiring. While he was not a pastor, he was a highly visible and respected figure. He talked to us about the need for "incarnational preaching," a concept which he described as getting into the culture so we could identify with the people.

To illustrate his point, the speaker related a personal story about raising his teenage sons. He described a recent Sunday morning on which his family was getting ready to go to church. They had just been through a stressful week at their house, and now they were at each other's throats while preparing to go to the Lord's house. It was a scenario that was all too familiar to many of us who were listening! He went on to describe his pastor's sermon for the morning. Sarcastically, he said the preacher "waxed eloquent" on an exposition from the Psalms about how to have an intimate relationship with God. The speaker confessed that he thought to himself as he left the service, *Well, Pastor, thank you very much. If I ever need to know about that, I'll have the information. But today I needed you to tell me how to raise my boys—and you didn't do it!* A host

1

of "Amens" rippled across the congregation as many of my fellow conference attendees vocalized their agreement.

The Questions Nobody Is Asking

On my trip home over the Atlantic, I had more than ten hours to process the speaker's assertion. While my heart resonated with the need for preaching to be relevant in our day, I struggled intensely with the inference that the driving force behind it ought to be the quest to answer all the questions people are asking. This struggle birthed a number of questions in my mind about the speaker's life situation. The first question was very practical—and personal. I wondered how I could possibly have answered the question that guy was asking had I been his pastor, especially in one sermon! I thought about the infinite number of variables involved in raising teenagers, not to mention the host of other life issues about which others in the congregation must have been curious that day. I have two teenage boys myself, and I know what it means to struggle. One of my struggles is that my boys are so radically different–ages, personalities, interests, temperaments, etc. I've got one son that I can punish very harshly, and he looks as if to say, "Is that all you've got?" I can just look at my other son sternly, however, and he melts in remorse! Throw into that mix all those other variables, and you discover that raising kids of any age is a tough row to hoe. I struggle with raising my own kids, much less telling somebody else how to raise theirs.

My second question grew out of the simple understanding of the preaching with which I was raised. I grew up believing that when the preacher got up to preach, his guiding responsibility was to speak "Thus saith the Lord;" therefore, I wondered whether or not the Bible provides the information our speaker desired. Do we have a definitive word from God about how to raise teenagers? I know what you're thinking: "Train up a child in the way he should go, and when he is old he will not depart from it" (Prov. 22:6); "Foolishness is bound up in the heart of a child, but the rod of correction will drive it far from him" (Prov. 22:15); "Do not provoke your children to wrath, but bring them up in the training and admonition of the Lord" (Eph. 6:4). But it's relatively safe to say that those were not the kind of answers for which my British friend was looking. Like church-goers everywhere, he was looking for *specific* and *practical* principles. But when you stop and think about it, the Bible really doesn't give us much information on the subject of raising teens. Does the Bible—the only source from which the preacher speaks with divine authority—address with specific and practical guidance all of the possible struggles plaguing us today? If not, where does the preacher get a definitive and authoritative word on these matters?

My struggle gravitated to a third question: What is the role and responsibility of my pastor as a preacher? Did God really commission him to be the dispenser of the infinite number of how-tos necessary for navigating daily life effectively? Is it possible for any preacher to be that smart? Can he be an expert in that many fields, especially when you consider the plethora of life issues for which people in the congregation are seeking help? Is it possible for any pastor to invest the kind of time necessary to research and organize such an expanse of information? There is no doubt in anyone's mind that today we churchgoers are asking questions about daily living. But are pastors responsible for or even capable of answering all of those questions?

This mental wrestling match culminated in the most important question of all: What is the purpose, or goal, of pastoral preaching? Is it really to answer all the questions that people are asking? Are those of us who preach failing our God, our calling, and our people if we neglect to do so? Are those of us who listen to preaching being neglected if we don't walk away from every sermon with a new set of practical instructions or the answers to our latest dilemma?

Although this tension was not new to me, this conference message sent me on a journey to help the average pastor and his parishioners answer these questions. I believe what I discovered will set many pastors free from the unrealistic expectations that are placed on them by contemporary cultures and congregations. Furthermore, what I discovered will enable those of us who listen to sermons to benefit from the message in ways that exceed merely having our questions answered. Where did I discover that freedom? Where else but in the ultimate preaching textbook—the Word of God.

The Question We Ought to Be Asking

Like many who have gone before me, I finally realized that preaching should not be driven by a preference, a program, or even a purpose, especially that of answering all the questions people ask. Instead, preaching should be driven by a passion for the glory of God, a passion jointly possessed by both pastor and people. The Bible is the story of how God ultimately is glorified in His redemptive plan to re-create mankind into His image, and the Scriptures are the Holy Spirit's primary agent for enacting that process. A preacher's call to preach is rooted in his call to Christ, and his call to Christ is rooted in a quest for the glory

3

of God. So, if his preaching is driven by anything other than a passion for the glory of God, it's being fueled by the wrong substance.

If our pursuit in coming to the sermon is primarily to see perceived needs met, to see all questions that are on the table answered, or even to give and receive practical help for daily living, then our journey ultimately will lead to someone or something other than God getting the glory. And usually it's the preacher or his philosophy that gets the credit. Preaching that is driven by a passion for the glory of God, however, always finds its target. Assuming the Bible is the only source from which the preacher speaks with the authority of God, such a passion frees the preacher to let the Bible simply say what it says—nothing more and nothing less.

So the ultimate question becomes, *How do we preach and listen to preaching in such a way as to bring glory to God, in each individual sermon and in the larger preaching ministry of our church?* Well, everyone knows that freedom comes with responsibility. The preaching pastor has a responsibility for handling the biblical text with integrity in order to ensure that he says only what God says. I believe such a responsibility manifests itself in one mandate for the pastor's primary weekly preaching ministry: *to rightly expose the mind of the Holy Spirit in every given text of Scripture.* Exposure to the truth of God's Word rightly unfolded is the only way that those of us who listen to sermons will ever be re-created into the image of Christ. And re-created people are one of the primary ways God is glorified in His church.

My hope and prayer for this book is that I can describe enough of my journey to inspire more preachers and listeners to be driven by a passion for God to be glorified. My limited thinking tells me that such a reformation must be built on three components: biblical foundation, philosophical framework, and practical implications. What we do normally is based upon what we believe, and what we believe ought to be based upon certain biblical principles or convictions. Part 1, "Passion-Driven Scripturology," is a study of a foundational Scripture passage, a popular exposition of 1 Corinthians 2:1–5. Here, the apostle Paul delineated certain convictions that formulated his practice of pastoral preaching, a practice which grew out of a passion for God's glory. Part 2, "Passion-Driven Shepherdology," is the development of selected themes which flow from these convictions and inform a philosophical framework for contemporary pastoral preaching for the glory of God. Part 3, "Passion-Driven Sermonology," simply offers some practical implications for pursuing the glory of God in the development, delivery, and reception of weekly sermons.

Each of the three chapters in each part corresponds to the respective chapters in the other two parts. The grid below helps to illustrate this unity. The (▼) symbol indicates the thematic development of each respective part as it relates to the content of preaching, the resource for preacher, and the goal in preaching. The (➡) symbol indicates the development of these subjects from biblical foundation to philosophical consideration to practical application.

Basically, this means that you can actually read the book one of two ways. If you want to follow the thematic development of the book, just read it vertically according to the chart above as you would most works, beginning with the first chapter and moving in succession all the way through the last chapter. If you prefer to follow the development of the *content*, for example, from biblical to philosophical to practical, then read it horizontally according to the chart below by beginning with the first chapter, then moving to the fourth chapter, and then to the seventh chapter. I will include a reminder of these options at the end of the pertinent chapters.

	PART 1 (Biblical)		PART 2 (Philosophical)		PART 3 (Practical)
(Content)	Chapter 1: The Message of Preaching ▼	➡	Chapter 4: The Shepherd's Stewardship ▼	➡	Chapter 7: Preaching as Worship ▼
(Resource)	Chapter 2: The Means for Preaching ▼	➡	Chapter 5: The Shepherd's Power ▼	➡	Chapter 8: Preaching with Potency ▼
(Goal)	Chapter 3: The Motive in Preaching	➡	Chapter 6: The Shepherd's Relevance	➡	Chapter 9: Preaching for Eternity

Part 1

PASSION-DRIVEN SCRIPTUROLOGY

Are you topical or textual? Deductive or inductive? Narrative or expository? Do you wear a tie or a golf shirt? Do you use a pulpit or a stool? Those kinds of questions might have been common among the preacher boys attending the Corinthian Bible College when Paul wrote 1 Corinthians. The seminary and denominational office bulletin boards were not filled with prayer requests for lost people or announcements about the next mission opportunity, but excerpts of articles highlighting contemporary preaching trends and the latest success stories. The question in everyone's mind when a preacher stood up to preach was not, *What word from the Lord does he bring?* but, *Which style does he use?* The pastor's conferences were not consumed with discussions about the evangelization of the city or the building up of the church but the relevance and application of the sermon. Yes, the church members in Corinth were the first real "party animals," and their preachers accommodated. Consequently, unsettledness and infighting characterized their church because members had developed a party spirit through their loyalties to certain preaching personalities and styles (see 1 Cor. 1:10–12). Sound familiar?

As Paul wrote to the Corinthian church, he must have done a mental roll call of the membership and used it to illustrate his point. He reminded them that not many of them had a whole lot of fame, wealth, education, power, or influence when they became Christians (see 1 Cor. 1:26). Paul always used the concept of *calling* to refer to the saving call of God that resulted in redemption. To be sure, the possession of such things is often the biggest factor in keeping people from an awareness of their need for salvation. Actually, it is the very feeling of inadequacy that is foundational for bringing people to an awareness of their need for the gospel (cf. Matt. 5:3; 11:25).

7

This paradoxical act of God is further developed in the next two verses. The secular culture of Paul's day viewed Christianity as foolishness. Not much has changed. The simplicity of the gospel and the humility with which it is to be shared by faithful believers is unfathomable to the world. But the economy of God is just the opposite of the world's thinking. What the world sees as foolishness is really wisdom, weakness shames the strong, and lowly status rises above high position (see 1 Cor. 1:27–28).

But don't be fooled. This irony of all ironies is not an accident but the very design of God to bring glory to Himself (see 1 Cor. 1:29–31). God changed all the price tags in the store window of the world so that nobody could get His glory. Now it was not because God sought the glory as if to seize something He didn't possess; He already has it! By nature all glory belongs to Him, and He wanted to ensure that no man would ever have a reason to steal what did not belong to him. That's why Paul said, "For by grace you have been saved through faith, and that not of yourselves; it is the gift of God, not of works, lest anyone should boast. For we are His workmanship" (Eph. 2:8–10).

The first five verses of 1 Corinthians 2 are at the very least the germination of the apostle Paul's approach to pastoral preaching. Some may argue that Paul's words here would be better applied to evangelistic, or even marketplace, preaching. Not according to Luke's account of Paul's initial ministry at Corinth: "He continued there a year and six months, teaching the word of God among them" (Acts 18:11). Based on recent studies in pastoral tenure, Paul was their pastor! Therefore, the study of this Scripture passage—this *scripturology*— reveals some key convictions he had about the pastor and his preaching, convictions that were birthed out of his passion for the glory of God.

*"And I, brethren, when I came to you, did not come with
excellence of speech or of wisdom declaring to you the
testimony of God. For I determined not to know anything
among you except Jesus Christ and Him crucified."*

1 CORINTHIANS 2:1–2

CHAPTER 1

The Message of Preaching:
GOD'S WORD VS. MAN'S WISDOM

Shortly after I had responded to God's call to preach, I remember a disturbing
event that would later have profound influence in shaping my understanding
and practice of preaching. I was privileged to serve as the associate to the pastor of a small country church who mentored me and gave me an opportunity to
stumble my way into Christian service. But, for various reasons, he was a somewhat discouraged man whose ministry had not developed the way he had
planned. Consequently, things between him and our congregation were not
good. There was tension in the church, and my mentor in ministry was bitter.

After a particularly stressful week, I remember him coming into the
Sunday morning worship service apparently distraught and frustrated. We
went through the announcements, songs of worship, offering, and special
music. Then, the pastor stepped up to the pulpit, placed his Bible on it, looked
out at the people, and announced, "I don't have a word from God this morning; God hasn't given me a word. Do any of you have a word?" The congregation was stone silent in shock. Then my pastor prayed and dismissed the
service. I was very green—like most young preachers—and did not know a
whole lot. For a few moments I sat on the front pew with my head down as
people were filing out. I just stared at the Bible I was gripping tightly with my
sweaty hands. And I remember as clear as day what I was thinking: *There are
sixty-six books of the Word of God in here, and you don't have a word from
God?* I didn't understand.

While I realize that my pastor's words were spoken out of deep distress, to
this day I cannot understand how a preacher could not have a word from God.
The apostle Paul was never without a word from God. He approached the
preaching event at Corinth in a way that was distinct from most of the other
preachers of his time. His claims in 1 Corinthians 2:1–2 are a beckon call for

9

pastoral preachers to make the Word of God primary in preaching content as opposed to the wisdom and ways of man. And those who listen to sermons must expect nothing more and nothing less.

The Preacher as Reporter

"The facts, ma'am, only the facts." I wish I had a dollar for every time I heard Sergeant Joe Friday, played by Jack Webb, say those words on the old television cop series *Dragnet*. The detective was always having to interrupt people he was interviewing in order to remind them that he needed only the facts of the story and not the rabbits they so frequently seemed to chase.

In one sense the preacher is a detective in hot pursuit of the facts and only the facts. But in a truer sense he is a *reporter* because he *reports* the facts when he finds them. The word translated *declaring* technically means "to report down" or "to proclaim throughout." Paul claimed to have come to Corinth *reporting* the facts, all the facts, and only the facts.

The Subject of the Report

Unlike many sermons today, the facts Paul *reported* were not regarding any and every subject under the sun. They were very specific, described as the "mystery" of God in the best manuscripts. In the Bible, this word does not mean something necessarily unknown but something not as fully understood at one time as it was at another. For Paul, the mystery was something not fully understood prior to the Christ event, but now it had been explained and illuminated by the Holy Spirit (see 1 Cor. 2:10–14). The concept is described in the following chapter as containing the wisdom of God and originating long before mankind ever arrived on the scene (see 1 Cor. 2:7). The preacher, then, is one who unfolds the mystery for his listeners under the guidance of God's Holy Spirit.

But while more manuscripts favor the word "mystery," some very good manuscripts render Paul's subject as a "testimony," which means "witness." The same word is mentioned in the previous chapter as that which was spoken by Christ and confirmed in the believers (see 1 Cor. 1:6). We really don't need to fret over whether *testimony* or *mystery* is the right term. In this passage they both describe the same thing—the message from God as revealed in the gospel. And they both imply the same criteria—"The facts, ma'am, only the facts." The detective seeks to solve the mystery with only the facts. The witness is bound to relay only the facts.

Before proceeding, I need to insert here a fundamental assumption that I will carry throughout this entire book. I firmly believe that in the larger scheme of the economy of God we do absolutely no injustice here by applying Paul's word—whether "mystery" or "testimony"—to the Holy Scriptures we have today called the Bible. If we go back to the Acts narrative regarding his ministry at Corinth, Luke told us that Paul "continued there a year and six months, teaching *the word of God* among them" (Acts 18:11, emphasis added). The "word of God" he taught certainly would have included Old Testament Scriptures (cf. Acts 13:13–41; 17:2,11; 28:23) and the apostles' doctrine (cf. Acts 2:42; 6:2–4; Eph. 2:20; 1 Cor. 12:28), as well as the revelation God was currently granting him as the primary inspired writer of our New Testament (cf. Gal. 1:11–2:2; 2 Pet. 3:14–16). Furthermore, the phrases "word of God" and "word of the Lord" are used twenty-one times in Acts, often interchangeably with references to the three sources mentioned above (e.g., Acts 11:16; 13:42–44, 48; 17:13).[1] There's no doubt that Paul would have seen the "testimony of God" and the "mystery of God" as being expressed in the Word of God.

When it comes to the *study* of the Word, I prefer the term "mystery." This word seems so much more appropriate for the preacher in his preparation as he seeks to uncover the facts of Scripture. But when he actually stands to *preach,* his speech is more conducive to a "testimony" of the facts. A testimony is essentially a witness, and a witness can tell only about what he or she has personally seen, heard, or experienced. Some time ago my wife was called to give a deposition in relation to an automobile accident. During the deposition, I listened as the lawyer asked what seemed like hundreds of questions that probed my wife's firsthand knowledge of the event. She was never asked about how she felt, what she thought, or the way in which she interpreted what transpired. She was asked only about the facts.

A witness in any legal forum is to recount only what he or she knows objectively, factually, and personally. The witness cannot speculate, guess, deduce, or conjecture. In Corinth, Paul provided a witness only of God's revelation in Christ as written in the Scriptures. It was not based on his own human understanding, reason, or inclinations. It was all about God's revelation because Paul knew that human wisdom amounted to nothing in the eternal scope of things.

Don't forget, however, that the passage does not say *Paul* was a witness, but that he merely came "declaring" as much. In other words, the preacher is not the witness himself; instead, he simply is called to *report* the facts given by the witness. Every time I turn on the television to watch the news, I see a host of men and women called *reporters* whose job it is to communicate the facts. They talk to witnesses, but they themselves merely report on the testimonies of the witnesses. News stations and newspapers are very careful to make a distinction between news reports and commentaries or editorials. While the latter contain opinions and interpretations, the former is supposed to be limited to *reporting* only the facts with no bias or opinions.

The Significance of the Report

Reporting about the work of God in Christ is found on a significant number of pages of the New Testament. Numerous times people spread the news about Jesus' incredible activity. After Jesus raised the ruler's daughter, "the *report* of this went out into all that land" (Matt. 9:26, emphasis added). After teaching and working miracles in Galilee, "Herod the tetrarch heard the *report* about Jesus" (Matt. 14:1, emphasis added). Upon rebuking a demon in the synagogue in Capernaum, "the *report* about Him went out into every place in the surrounding region" (Luke 4:37, emphasis added). When He healed a man with leprosy, "the *report* went around concerning Him all the more" (Luke 5:15, emphasis added). And in response to His raising the dead son of the widow of Nain, "this *report* about Him went throughout all Judea and all the surrounding region" (Luke 7:17, emphasis added).

The most vivid pictures, however, are found in those references which have direct relationship to the preaching event. Twice in the New Testament reference is made to the fulfillment of the great messianic text, Isaiah 53. Regarding the proclamation of the coming Messiah, Isaiah had posed the question, "Who has believed our *report*?" (Isa. 53:1, emphasis added). John indicated that the refusal of the Jews to believe Jesus' testimony about Himself even though He had done many signs in their midst was so "that the word of Isaiah the prophet might be fulfilled, which he spoke: 'Lord, who has believed our *report*?'" (John 12:38, emphasis added).

The second connection to Isaiah's prophecy is made by the apostle Paul himself in his letter to the Romans. In the midst of that great missionary text in Romans 10:14–21 in which he magnifies the role of preaching in the propagation of the gospel, Paul said, "But they have not all obeyed the gospel. For Isaiah says, 'Lord, who has believed our *report*?'" (Rom. 10:16, emphasis added). When Isaiah spoke the words quoted by Paul here and by John above, the prophet was speaking of the suffering, dying work of the Savior as noted in Isaiah 53:5, who

> *was* wounded for our transgressions,
> *He was* bruised for our iniquities;

The chastisement for our peace *was* upon Him,
And by His stripes we are healed.

The *report* of which Isaiah and Paul spoke is the good news of the crucified Christ, the glad tidings of His substitutionary death that we might live. That is what preachers are to *report*.

Paul saw *reporting* the truth of God as his only task, and so it would seem the task of every preacher. Any other approach is a prostitution of the preaching ministry. The apostle had already assured the Corinthians that he had not invaded their midst with human thoughts and opinions, but only the testimony of God. He later affirmed this commitment when he wrote, "But we have renounced the hidden things of shame, not walking in craftiness nor handling the word of God deceitfully, but by manifestation of the truth commending ourselves to every man's conscience in the sight of God" (2 Cor. 4:2). To his young protege in the ministry, Timothy, he warned, "Now the Spirit expressly says that in latter times some will depart from the faith, giving heed to deceiving spirits and doctrines of demons, speaking lies in hypocrisy, having their own conscience seared with a hot iron" (1 Tim. 4:1–2). The young pastor was charged to "give attention to reading, to exhortation, to doctrine" (1 Tim. 4:13) and to "preach the word" both "in season and out of season" (2 Tim. 4:1–2). It is incomprehensible that any man who calls himself one of God's shepherds would do anything else but *report* what God has said.

The Source of the Report

The nature of the facts and from whence they come are also important for the *reporter*. So Paul was specific about the source and the subject of his message. The context of the passage seems to suggest that the possessive "of God" (1 Cor. 2:1) is subjective, suggesting that Paul's message was the testimony that God gave inasmuch as it had God as its content. While the context of the passage reveals that this message certainly had God as its subject, the apostle unapologetically claimed that his message actually originated with God.

During the celebrated O. J. Simpson trial of 1995, a controversy arose over some taped phone conversations involving Los Angeles police detective Mark Fuhrman. Fuhrman, the officer who found the bloody glove at Simpson's estate the day after the murder of his ex-wife, reportedly made racist comments on the tapes and referred to alleged incidents of police brutality by the Los Angeles Police Department. During the proceedings on September 5, before Judge Lance Ito had decided whether or not to admit the tapes as evidence, a woman walked to the front of the courtroom's spectator area with a large envelope. She raised the envelope and said in a loud voice, "Judge Ito, Judge Ito, I have a message for you from God. God wants you to play the tapes." This lady did not primarily claim to have a message *about* God but one that both originated with Him and belonged to Him.

That's what Paul did. He was not merely claiming to have a message *about* God. He walked into the pagan city of Corinth and said, "Corinthians, Corinthians, I have a message for you *from* God." And he knew that message was the only thing that would reveal the truth about life and eternity, and he gave God the credit. In other words, his passion for God's glory determined the content of his preaching. He went to great pains to ensure that what he put on the table for his listeners was, in fact, the very Word of God as opposed to the mere wisdom of man. So Paul's message was *from* God and *about* God. And all Christian *reporting* should be of like kind—communicating the revelation that is both *about* and *from* God.

Most preachers today, however, do not have a problem preparing and delivering sermons that are *about* God. It is the *from* part that is often absent. There is a subtle yet significant difference between preaching content that originates with God and that which is merely *about* Him. It seems that in our day preaching is validated on the basis of its relational proximity to the concept of God, Christian living, moral character, and even just good practical advice. While we will tackle this issue more thoroughly in a later chapter, suffice it to say now that not all good and helpful information is necessarily that which God intended His preachers to *report*. He has given to us a specific message to deliver, and that message does not always include all things helpful, good, and God-related. The message with which preachers have been entrusted is the very Word of God— nothing more, nothing less. And those who listen to preaching are obligated to desire the same.

The Preacher as Reminder

It took me a long time to succumb to the peer pressure of getting a personal digital assistant (PDA), but finally I yielded. Everybody had them. I would sit in meetings and colleagues on both sides of me would be scribbling notes with their styluses and beaming them to one another. Across the room, another individual would be typing away on one of those portable keyboards. I love toys, but I just could not see the advantage of giving up my trusty DayTimer for another electronic fad. But the first time I played with a friend's device sitting on an airplane, I was hooked. And after performing my first "HotSync" operation when I purchased my own unit, I became the top promoter for the company!

Of all the cool features my handheld possesses, I have probably benefitted most from the little "alarm" feature on my date book. My DayTimer never used to talk to me. But when I enter an appointment or an event into my PDA date book, I can attach a *reminder* to it. I can even determine how far in advance I want to be *reminded*. At the appointed time, a little alarm of three short beeps will go off *reminding* me of the event. And the really neat part is that it will just keep going off about every ten minutes or so until I acknowledge that I have been *reminded*! Our text under consideration suggests that Paul believed that the preacher is not only a reporter but a *reminder* of that which has been reported.

The Task of Reminding

The Christian preacher is commissioned with a particular task, that of *reminding* people over and over again of God's Word and its claim on their lives. We find this theme often in the New Testament, from both Paul and others. Paul told the Romans, "Nevertheless, brethren, I have written more boldly to you on some points, as *reminding* you, because of the grace given to me by God" (Rom. 15:15, emphasis added). To the Philippians he wrote, "Finally, my brethren, rejoice in the Lord. For me to write the same things to you is not tedious, but for you it is safe" (Phil. 3:1). Even Jude got in on the action and said, "But I want to *remind* you, though you once knew this, that the Lord, having saved the people out of the land of Egypt, afterward destroyed those who did not believe" (Jude 5, emphasis added).

The apostle Peter probably filled the bill more than any other New Testament writer. He seemed to place a huge amount of emphasis on the preacher as *reminder*. In one passage he *reminded* us about *reminding* three times:

> For this reason I will not be negligent to *remind* you always of these things, though you know and are established in the present truth. Yes, I think it is right, as long as I am in this tent, to stir you up by *reminding* you, knowing that shortly I must put off my tent, just as our Lord Jesus Christ showed me. Moreover I will be careful to ensure that you always have a *reminder* of these things after my decease (2 Pet. 1:12–15, emphasis added).

And again in another place:

> Beloved, I now write to you this second epistle (in both of
> which I stir up your pure minds by way of *reminder*), that you
> may be mindful of the words which were spoken before by the
> holy prophets, and of the commandment of us, the apostles of
> the Lord and Savior (2 Pet. 3:1–2, emphasis added).

Obviously, many of the New Testament writers saw themselves as responsible for *reminding* God's people about things they had previously been told. They knew it was necessary if the human mind was ever going to embrace the truth and enable it to sink into the heart.

The Topic of Reminding

But of what exactly did Paul *remind* the Corinthians? To be sure, when he said in 1 Corinthians 2:2, "I determined not to know anything among you except," he put some pretty narrow parameters on his preaching topic. This claim almost suggests that Paul would have had to commit what some consider to be the unpardonable sin of delivering the same sermon over and over again! If that is the case, it must have been a doozie! And so it was. His "testimony of God" is specified in the phrase "Jesus Christ and Him crucified" (vv. 1–2). This was Paul's preaching topic in a nutshell! This is what he *reminded* the Corinthians of over and over. It was in fact a doozie of a message—the ultimate sugar stick sermon! In fact, this message *from* God was so important that Paul gave lesser roles to factors such as oratorical ability and thought processes in order to feature it in his preaching.

When you have a message from God instead of just the wisdom of man, it is worth preaching over and over again. Paul refused to dedicate one second of time to a discussion of men's ideas or insights, including his own. His sermons were consumed with the crucifixion, resurrection, and redemption of Jesus Christ. And Paul wanted us to know that he did not merely set Jesus up as the perfect teacher or the perfect example of what a man ought to be. While Jesus certainly was all of these and more, Paul constantly *reminded* his listeners that Jesus of Nazareth was both Savior and God who had earned the right to lay claim on every person's life.

Such has been the heartbeat of Christian proclamation since Pentecost. The proposition and culmination of that first Christian sermon was set forth when Peter said, "Therefore let all the house of Israel know assuredly that God has made this Jesus, whom you crucified, both Lord and Christ" (Acts 2:36). He and the other apostles continued to resound the same message in the coming days, saying that "the God of our fathers raised up Jesus whom you murdered by hanging on a tree. Him God has exalted to His right hand *to be* Prince and Savior, to give repentance to Israel and forgiveness of sins" (Acts 5:30–31).

When you stop and think about it, the lordship and saviorhood of Jesus Christ is the most significant and relevant issue for people in contemporary culture for at least two reasons. First, it is where all eternity is headed. After describing Jesus' humility in submitting Himself to the death of the cross, Paul said that "God also has highly exalted Him and given Him the name which is above every name, that at the name of Jesus every knee should bow, of those in heaven, and of those on earth, and of those under the earth, and *that* every tongue should confess that Jesus Christ *is* Lord, to the glory of God the Father" (Phil. 2:9–11). All of eternity is going to wind up bowing at the feet of the Lord Jesus Christ, all because of His saving act! Second, it is the only way anyone can head for eternity. Paul said to the Romans, "If you confess with your mouth the Lord Jesus and believe in your heart that God has raised Him from the dead, you will be saved" (Rom. 10:9). Salvation from sin, death, and eternal separation from God can be found only in the crucified Christ.

From beginning to end our Bible is a book about the Christ event. Jesus Himself claimed not to have come "to destroy the Law or the Prophets . . . but to fulfill" (Matt. 5:17). He told the religious hypocrites of His day, "You search the Scriptures, for in them you think you have eternal life; and these are they which testify of Me" (John 5:39). To the disciples on the road to Emmaus, "beginning at Moses and all the Prophets, He expounded to them in all the Scriptures the things concerning Himself" (Luke 24:27). Charles Spurgeon said that he would begin at any point in the Bible and make a beeline for the cross. Maybe Katherine Hankey summarized best what ought to be the confession of every preacher when she wrote:

> I love to tell the story; 'tis pleasant to repeat
> What seems each time I tell it, more wonderfully sweet:
> I love to tell the story, for some have never heard
> The message of salvation from God's own holy Word.
>
> I love to tell the story; for those who know it best
> Seem hungering and thirsting to hear it like the rest:
> And when, in scenes of glory, I sing the new, new song,
> 'Twill be the old, old story that I have loved so long.
>
> *I love to tell the story, 'Twill be my theme in glory*
> *To tell the old, old story of Jesus and his love.*

If you are looking for a camp to be in when it comes to preaching trends, camp out on the "old, old story." Such is part of the mystery of preaching—the consistent *reminder* of the crucified Christ.

The Tension of Reminding

There is a very real tension, however, that the preacher as reminder must navigate. Certainly not everyone today recognizes the importance and relevance of the Christ event. Nor did they in Paul's day. Yet he made it the heart of his preaching even though he knew it was a "stumbling block" to the Jews and "foolishness" to the Greeks (1 Cor. 1:23; cf. Gal. 6:14). To be sure, the cross always offends! While the crucified Christ is a familiar concept to us, it remains a foolish and offensive idea to the world.

Sometimes the foolishness and offense of this message comes about because of familiarity and frequency. *Reminding* suggests repetition, and many preachers are afraid of repetition. In fact, it seems that many contemporary preachers shy away from the role of *reminder* because of the fear of repetition in the pulpit. As I listen to some preachers today, I get the impression that they feel like they have to come up with something new every week that no one else has ever come up with before. And the aversion to repetition on the part of many listeners as well as their expectations of "new material" doesn't help. The spirit of the Epicureans and Stoics has found its way into the pulpit and the pew, "for all the Athenians and the foreigners who were there spent their time in nothing else but either to tell or to hear some new thing" (Acts 17:21).

This fear of repetition combined with an affinity for "fresh stuff" impacts preaching adversely in a number of areas. For example, it sometimes causes preachers to maximize secondary application and minimize the primary intent of certain passages. In the Gospel of John, for instance, the writer is very clear that his purpose in recording the events in the narrative was so "that you may believe that Jesus is the Christ, the Son of God, and that believing you may have life in His name" (John 20:31). Even though every passage in this Gospel is not necessarily directly addressed to unbelievers, the preacher is responsible for approaching—and preaching—every passage with this understanding. The fear of repeating the same thing over and over again forces many preachers to resort to secondary application of various passages without ever even acknowledging the overarching evangelistic intent in relation to the larger purpose of the gospel.

Another example of maximizing secondary application and minimizing primary intent is the failure to follow the purpose of various miracle passages in the Gospels. A large number of those events were intended to validate the deity of Jesus. Consider Mark 4:35–41, for instance, where Jesus calms the sea. Close consideration of the text reveals that such a supernatural feat could be accomplished only by God Himself. The physical quieting of creation is something only God can do! But an aversion to repeating the proof of Jesus' deity in the Gospel forces many preachers to allegorize the passage and talk about the "storms of life." The fear of repetition leads us to promote a hermenuetical paradigm that we would otherwise shun!

The fact of the matter is that the Gospels (and the gospel!) are textbooks in repetition. They are called the "Gospels" for a reason—because they primarily are about the good news of the crucified Christ, not about the daily plight of mankind. And for some reason God determined that we needed four of them! Maybe it's because He knew that repetition is the pathway to learning!

The aversion to repetition also affects preaching adversely by creating a fear of systematic series. Some preachers refuse to preach through books because of the necessity to stay with a particular theme for an extended period of time. Also, systematic series usually require some degree of "review" each week in order to establish the connection between individual passages. A preacher's neglect of such an approach robs the church of an important aspect of Bible teaching, a subject we will address in more detail later.

Probably the biggest tension created by the call for repetition in preaching comes in the pastoral pulpit. Many pastors shrink from preaching Christ and the cross because of the *awkwardness* of saying the same thing over and over to basically the same group of people. This element of awkwardness exists with all true gospel preaching. In the local church especially, a pastor will be preaching to some of the same faces week after week and year after year. The awkwardness sets in when that sameness is coupled with the biblical demand to continually preach the familiar theme—the crucified Christ.

I, along with many others in our community, enjoy walking and running for exercise. The oval-shaped perimeter of our seventy-five-acre campus in New Orleans makes a great exercise area, and people are always moving around it in both directions. If you have ever made laps around a track, a gym, or in some other kind of circular pattern, you probably have experienced an awkwardness that I frequently encounter. Do you know what the toughest part is for me? It's not the discipline it takes to get out and do it. It's not having enough strength or breathe to complete the laps. It's not even the frustration of trying to determine whether or not it's doing any good. The toughest part of that whole deal is trying to figure out creative ways to greet the same people moving in the opposite direction every time you pass them! We have to be honest here. There are only so many ways to sincerely greet the same people within a ten- to twenty-minute time period. And depending on where you enter the circle, you might pass the same people just going around once or twice. This is a real problem!

Now my limited observation has led me to conclude that people respond to this awkwardness in three ways. Some of the serious health nuts never acknowledge that anyone else is on the planet! Or, if they do, they stop acknowledging them after the first greeting on the first lap. It's as if they were on a mission for God, and no one or nothing else matters. Others, who are more recreational in their journey, make small talk after the first greeting which serves as a token acknowledgment. After the first lap on which they say "Hello," "Hey," or "Hi," they offer comments like, "Beautiful weather today, huh?" "Nice shorts!" or "How 'bout those New Orleans Saints?" But there are always those social exercisers who find a variety of creative ways to offer a token greeting every time they pass you. They wave, they nod, they speak, all in a potpourri of attempts to be cordial. All three of these responses are simple attempts by human beings to overcome the awkwardness of repetition.

While figuring out how to greet people doing laps creates some element of tension, choosing how to respond to the awkwardness of gospel preaching in the local church is a far tougher and more important assignment. But the options are the same. First, the pastor can stop talking about Christ and the cross after he's been on the field for a short while. That would be apostasy. Second, he can make small talk in the pulpit with extrabiblical material clothed in "practical and relevant" rhetoric, giving only token acknowledgment to the person and work of Jesus. That would be compromise. There is a difference between Jesus as a good example or pattern and Jesus as the crucified Lord who lays claim to every person's life. Third, the pastoral preacher can find creative ways from the plethora of biblical literature to preach the same old story of the crucified Lord and His claims on the lives of people. For Paul and for us, only the third option is acceptable.

The Preacher as Reflector

When driving for long periods of time on the interstate, I often find my mind wandering out of sheer boredom. I start doing the weirdest things. Sometimes I find a dirty spot or a mashed bug on the windshield, then see if I can use my line of sight to weave it (the bug, not the vehicle) in and out of the dashed lines in the middle of the road without touching them. I guess it's just the competitor within me! At other times, however, I am much more practical. For example, I cannot even begin to count the number of times I have found myself coveting the patent on those little reflectors that line both sides of every inch of interstate across the entire country. How would you like to be the guy who came up with that idea?

Reality is that those simple little objects are paramount for the safety and well-being of drivers and passengers. They make it possible to navigate an otherwise dark path. In the same way, the preacher is a *reflector* each week when he stands to preach the Word of God. He is responsible for providing listeners with the light of the gospel which is necessary for navigating the otherwise dark path of a sinful world. So the stakes are even higher when it comes to the safety and well-being of those who listen to preaching.

Reflection of the Cross

Those little reflectors are simple things—like the hula hoop and Slinky—that made somebody very rich. The guy who came up with the reflector idea didn't even have to discover electricity, or lights, or anything like that! Somebody else had to come up with the tough, detailed stuff. This guy just invented something that used some other source of light, and he developed something that makes a big difference in the lives of a whole lot of people in a whole lot of different ways. There are reflectors on roads, on signs, on bicycles, on cars—they are everywhere. There are literally thousands upon thousands of applications of the reflector.

Neither does the preacher have to come up with the source of light that he *reflects.* Somebody else has already done that. That "somebody" is the crucified Christ, the light of the world. The preacher simply is responsible for *reflecting* the light. What drives the preacher's *reflection,* then, is not anything that emanates from the culture or the audience, but that which emanates from the cross of Jesus Christ. And that says volumes about the content of preaching today.

Contemporary preachers must understand that the light of the cross has not faded or given way to new sources of illumination. In the language of the New Testament, the perfect participle "crucified" (1 Cor. 2:2) indicates that not only was Christ once crucified, but He continues in the character of the crucified One.[2] That means the effect and nature of the crucified Christ still has bearing on every person's life today, both Christian and non-Christian. In other words, this message is timeless because the implications of the crucified Christ remain the single most significant need in people's lives in every generation, for Christians as well as non-Christians!

The timelessness of the crucified Christ demands that our messages be focused on Him and not us. In other words, preaching should be rooted in a call to the crucified life. When you look closely, Paul's letters to the churches were *reflections* on and applications of the gospel message he had preached in the beginning. This text indicates that even though Paul knew that his audience considered his message "foolishness," he still preached the crucified Christ (see 1 Cor. 1:22–23) as "a direct challenge to an alternative way of viewing reality."[3] He did not primarily attempt to respond to the questions that people were asking, nor did he make any attempt to present Christianity as the answer to their own personal pursuits. The claim that God had acted in the Christ event flew in the face of the culture's myths in a scandalous way!

Most pastors and congregants assume such as the nature of *evangelistic* preaching. But if cross-centered preaching that counters the whims of the culture is right for *evangelistic* efforts, why should preaching to *believers* be of such a radically different nature? Where do we get the idea that once we become Christians our whims and desires suddenly become the all-supreme determinant of what the preacher is to preach? It seems that no longer is it the claims of the Christ-life that set the preaching agenda but the questions of man's life. According to our text, the life that was crucified to save us from our sins is the same life that is necessary for us to navigate holiness in a fallen world. Peter said, "Grace and peace be multiplied to you in the knowledge of God and of Jesus our Lord, as His divine power has given to us all things that *pertain* to life and godliness, through the knowledge of Him who called us by glory and virtue" (2 Pet. 1:2–3). It is in knowing Him that those of us who listen to sermons know how to live life.

This is not at all foreign to the beckoning call of the New Testament. Jesus Himself said, "'If anyone desires to come after Me, let him deny himself, and take up his cross daily, and follow Me. For whoever desires to save his life will lose it, but whoever loses his life for My sake will save it'" (Luke 9:23–24). Paul said his goal was to "know Him and the power of His resurrection, and the fellowship of His sufferings, being conformed to His death" (Phil. 3:10). Both taking up the cross daily and being conformed to His death suggest a timeless application of the crucified Christ.

Not all but much of the "felt needs" and "life situation" preaching of our day serves as an illustration here. While claiming to have Christ as its theme, it offers practical help for dealing with the human situation without ever revealing the claims of Jesus Christ on human life and without presenting His life as the ultimate solution to man's problems. "Felt needs" preaching often addresses the questions of listeners but never introduces them to a holy God in Christ. Consequently, people frequently leave our services with practical help for their life situation but with no better understanding of the powerful help that comes only through carrying their cross. They often leave understanding more about themselves but no more about a holy God. This kind of preaching causes man and his needs to overshadow the message of the cross, and all the attention goes to either the preacher or the people—but not to God. Preacher, every sermon you preach ought to *reflect* the crucified Christ onto the lives of your listeners. And listeners, you need to be looking for that light, not any source of illumination that might emanate from other sources.

Reflection on the Church

I learned an important lesson about people's perception of preaching shortly after assuming my second pastorate, a small congregation in the deep south. I began immediately preaching systematically through a book of the Bible. All of the messages during the first several weeks were more fellowship-oriented, addressing Christians as the respective texts demanded. I assumed the people were receiving the sermons eagerly as their shepherd fed them the Word. Boy, was I naive! About two months into the series, I finally came to a text that was more evangelistic in nature. So I proceeded on Sunday morning to wax eloquent with a hot sermon on hell, making primary application to those persons without Christ. The next day one of the prominent men in the church stopped in front of my house as I was mowing the lawn. He rolled down the window of his truck and yelled, "Great message yesterday, Pastor. You finally started preaching!" And I thought I had been *preaching* all along.

The fact of the matter is that many congregations today believe that every sermon ought to be directed at the lost, informing them of their sinful condition and their eternal destiny of torment. And, in the minds of many, the preacher is not preaching until he has done so. Sadly, however, many of those same parishioners would never lift a finger to make sure a lost person was there to hear it. Equally as tragic is the reality that so many Christians today do not see the value of preaching for their daily lives or even their maturity in Christ.

So the role of the preacher as *reflector* of the cross raises an interesting dilemma in weekly preaching. Is every sermon of every week supposed to be a salvation message? When Paul said he preached nothing but the crucified Christ, was he admitting that he preached nothing but evangelistic messages?

Did he sermonize only those parts of Scripture that dealt directly with Christ's atonement?

The answer to that question is a resounding "No!" We must understand that preaching the crucified Christ is not necessarily synonymous with preaching evangelistic sermons. Paul was keenly aware that the person and work of Jesus the Messiah comprise the entire gospel—including the resurrection (see 1 Cor. 15:1–11)—as well as its implications for the Christian life. Think about it. The very epistle under consideration here, along with the host of others penned by Paul, is a testimony to the fact that he was not limiting his understanding of the crucified Christ to the simple plan of salvation. He wrote to *churches*! To be sure, Paul taught the full counsel of God (see Acts 18:11; 20:27) in his preaching of Christ crucified.

The shepherd of the local congregation has the responsibility of *reflecting* weekly on the cross of Christ in order to show its implications and applications for the body of Christ and the individuals who comprise it. That is what the majority of the New Testament is—a *reflection* and application of the gospel as recorded in Matthew, Mark, Luke, and John! And the *reflection* of the cross of Christ has an infinite number of implications and applications for God's people. Just like the reflectors mentioned above, these applications are everywhere— on families, students, singles, divorcees, grandparents, churches, nations, and so on. Everybody and just about everything needs to have the light of the crucified Christ *reflected* on it!

Reflection of a Conviction

Before leaving this subject, one other issue needs to be settled. It's a personal issue for the preacher—one he must decide for himself. I'm speaking of the personal conviction to *reflect* only the message of the cross to the church. Every preacher will have to choose whether or not he will preach only Christ and Him crucified as revealed on the pages of the Bible. And be aware, that is a conviction that can only be established by faith. While there is much historical and scientific evidence that points to the validity of the Bible and the Christ it reveals, there remains a gap that can be bridged only by the faith of the preacher.

G. Campbell Morgan, the Prince of Expositors, once suffered a personal crisis fostered by some of the critical theories of his day. It plunged him into the darkness of doubt. Setting aside all his books, he set out to discover for himself if the Bible was indeed what it claimed to be. When all was said and done, he found his faith and his conviction. More importantly, as he said, "The Bible found me."[4] His conviction birthed a preaching ministry that impacted two continents and, through his writings, continues to bless Christians worldwide.

The Christ of the Scriptures had found Paul. To ensure that he presented his message for God's glory, Paul willfully chose not to be distracted with lesser subjects in his preaching, but to *reflect* only the crucified Christ in his preaching. Many great preachers have wrestled with issues regarding their convictions about the Word. But no great preacher has ever carried such a struggle throughout his ministry.

We may never know if, when, or how long Paul struggled with determining the content of his preaching. What we do know is that the issue had been settled when he got off the bus in Corinth. In the language of the New Testament, the verb "determined" (1 Cor. 2:2) is in the aorist tense, indicating a fact which had come to its conclusion. In other words, preaching only Christ and Him crucified was something the apostle had decided before ever arriving on the church field. He did not wait until he arrived to determine what to preach. He did not wait for some tingling feeling or mystical impression before he could get a sermon. His content was not dependent upon the results of recent audience analysis or the latest demographic research. He did not even have to wait until he got to know the people. Paul had settled the issue of what his preaching content would be long before he ever stepped into the pulpit at Corinth. And that message was both Scripture-driven and Christocentric.

Many scholars believe that it was Paul's perceived misfortune at Athens (cf. Acts 17:16–34) that led him to such a decision, suggesting that he had attempted some other approach. More likely is the belief that the events on Mars Hill merely served to confirm Paul's commitment as opposed to changing his philosophy of preaching. A closer consideration of the Acts narrative reveals several factors that support as much. First, Paul did not get to finish his sermon but was cut off at the mention of the resurrection. Second, Paul began his sermon with a biblical presentation of creation and ended it with the resurrection. Needless to say, discussion of the resurrection implies discussion of the crucifixion and provides a fairly close connection to "Jesus Christ and Him crucified." Third, some in the audience that day believed Paul's message and joined his company (see Acts 17:34). And since there is no other name under heaven given among men by which we can be saved, Paul must have preached the death, burial, and resurrection of Jesus at some point.

So what does that mean for us today? Somewhere in the preacher's ministry (ideally before he begins to preach), he will have to decide the issue of content in his preaching. He will have to make a willful decision to stick with the message of the book—Jesus Christ and Him crucified. If not, he will be tossed to and fro, from trend to trend, and carried about by every wind of preaching doctrine. And while his preaching may be characterized by the norms of contemporary rhetoric aimed at the newest discoveries of audience analysis and generational surveys, it will not contain the only thing that is potent enough to supernaturally transform lives.

The authority of the preacher lies solely in the authority of his message. That is both a blessing and a privilege. So preachers ought never to abuse the privilege or minimize the blessing. He does not have to spend the valuable time of his ministry trying to convince people of his own authority through cosmopolitan delivery or supposed "relevant" content that comes from outside the Bible. He can simply rest in the authority of the One who sent him. Rather than relegating preaching to the opinions and ideas of men, he can boldly proclaim, "Thus saith the Lord."

When the authority of the Word becomes prominent in the pulpit ministry of the church, both preacher and listeners will experience the wonder and awe of being fellow laborers with God, reaching people and seeing lives changed. And as a man of God preaches out of a deep conviction that the Bible is the fully matured message of the crucified Christ, those of us who listen will receive the message more seriously and consider it more binding as the power of God works mightily through the preaching event.[5]

Billy Graham made a journey similar to that of G. Campbell Morgan. Early in his ministry he found himself questioning whether or not the Bible was indeed the Word of God. At the end of an agonizing spiritual pilgrimage, he resolved to preach the Bible as God's Word to man.[6] His piercing statement "The Bible says" continues to ring across the globe and reflects the determination he made to preach Christ alone. When you approach the Bible seriously and prayerfully, you may have to wrestle with it for a time. But do not throw in the towel. The victory that awaits will enable you to know, preach and hear Christ and Him crucified. Then He'll get all the glory!

Where Do I Go from Here . . .

Now that you have begun this journey into a practical theology of pastoral preaching, you may proceed one of two ways as indicated by the shaded areas on the chart below. The (▼) symbol indicates the thematic development of the remainder of Paul's approach to preaching as revealed in 1 Corinthians 2:1–5. If you choose this path, proceed to chapter 2, "The Means for Preaching." The

(➡) symbol indicates the continued development of the *content* of preaching from philosophical and then practical standpoints. If you choose this path, proceed to chapter 4, "The Shepherd's Stewardship." Before beginning chapter 4, however, be sure to read the introduction to part 2, "Passion-Driven Shepherdology."

Table 1.1

	PART 1 (Biblical)		PART 2 (Philosophical)		PART 3 (Practical)
(Content)	Chapter 1: The Message of Preaching ▼	➡	Chapter 4: The Shepherd's Stewardship ▼	➡	Chapter 7: Preaching as Worship ▼
(Resource)	Chapter 2: The Means for Preaching ▼	➡	Chapter 5: The Shepherd's Power ▼	➡	Chapter 8: Preaching with Potency ▼
(Goal)	Chapter 3: The Motive in Preaching	➡	Chapter 6: The Shepherd's Relevance	➡	Chapter 9: Preaching for Eternity

"And I, brethren, when I came to you, did not come with excellence of speech or of wisdom declaring to you the testimony of God. For I determined not to know anything among you except Jesus Christ and Him crucified. I was with you in weakness, in fear, and in much trembling. And my speech and my preaching were not with persuasive words of human wisdom, but in demonstration of the Spirit and of power."

1 Corinthians 2:1–4

CHAPTER 2

The Means for Preaching:

God's Power vs. Man's Presentation

I think I'm going to print a T-shirt that I believe could potentially make me a rich man. On it will be one simple phrase—*It's all about me!* I think people would buy it. Why? Because it's the motto of our culture. It's the "life verse" of humanity. Everywhere you go and in every aspect of society, people talk and act like the entire world revolves around them, many times with a total disregard for the wishes and even safety of others. When I go to the grocery store in my city, automobiles fill the fire lane as their owners attempt to get closer to the door so they don't have to walk as far. When the light turns green at an intersection, you better count to five before proceeding, or you are likely to get broadsided by someone racing through the red light on the cross street. Consciously or unconsciously, many people believe, *It's all about me!*

Maybe Christians—and especially preachers—should counter the culture with a different T-shirt. On the front it could simply read, *It's not about me . . . .* And on the back it could read, *It's all about Him!* That was the banner Paul waved. Having settled the issue of preaching content in his heart and mind, he refused to present his message in a way that was dependant upon the empowerment of wise and persuasive arguments, personal popularity and ability, or any other form of self-reliance. Although he came in a very unostentatious way, he was able to display genuine spiritual power because of the work of God's Spirit in and through him. Such should be the confession of preachers in every age so that only God gets the glory in their preaching. After all, it *is* all about Him.

The Priority in Preaching

"Provocative images fill the TV screen. Over a driving, syncopated rock beat, a woman's voice—urgent, seductive—tells a story of possession and salvation."[1] A commentary on the latest Britney Spears music video? Not quite. Try a news magazine's review of a contemporary video rendition of the Luke 8 passage when Jesus cast out the host of demons from the man of Gadara. The *Time* magazine reviewer summarized: The "message is overwhelmed by the medium."

Could educator Marshall McLuhan actually have been right when he proposed that "the medium is the message" in his 1967 work by the same name? Can *how* we say something affect people as much as *what* we say? Paul seemed to think so. Consequently, he went to great lengths to make sure that his message was always given top priority in the preaching event.

The Feature in Christian Communication

The apostle Paul was careful to ensure that nothing was ever allowed to cancel out his message. In other words, he determined to always feature the message in his communication. In order to prevent anything from usurping his message, Paul intentionally avoided any dependence on fine dialectical oration, striking speculative thought, and other qualities of secular communication.

Now don't miss this. The word *excellence* (1 Cor. 2:1) in the passage means "rising out above" and carries the idea of having preeminence or superiority.[2] The word is used to characterize both the way the message is presented— "speech"—and the way in which the mind coordinates the message—"wisdom." Both of these ideas inform the presentation of the preacher's message. Be sure to notice that Paul did not say he refused to utilize good speech, nor did he say that he never gave attention to his thought processes or those of his listeners. He simply claimed never to allow those realities to overshadow—or *rise out above*—the message in the presentation of the sermon.

Many preachers today face the temptation to obscure the content of their message in order to make it more palatable to contemporary audiences. Obscurity often occurs when the means of the presentation or the nature of a given audience are stressed to the point of *rising out above* the message of the Bible. One of the biggest struggles we preachers will have in the pulpit is to employ a manner of presentation that might naturally seem to appeal more to a given audience and then to put such emphasis on it that it veils what really is important. And many times we as listeners are demanding such in sermons!

Let me insert something at this point that is very difficult for a preacher— and especially a teacher of preaching—to admit. One of the things that is most often overlooked in discussions about preaching is the fact that preaching is only a means to an end. The message is what matters! So when the preacher's method of presentation or the way in which the human mind manages information is emphasized to such a degree that it overshadows the message itself, the preacher commits spiritual treason. A rebellion takes place that results in the abdication of the throne in preaching to a lesser influence.

Paul's claim here is incredible in light of many contemporary preaching trends that place a large amount of emphasis on preaching style as well as the nature of the "thought processes" of both preacher and listener. I hear and read much discussion today about things like conversational speech, relational presentations, right-brain and left-brain thinking, oral culture, visual age, the postmodern mind-set, and other considerations that often are championed as the supreme, all-important determinants of how we should preach. And while all of these considerations should be given their due value in the preaching event, the Bible seems to suggest that they must never be allowed to reign supreme.

The Form of Christian Communication

It is also important to note that Paul did not take his cue on speaking to the culture from secular public orators. Commenting on the video presentation mentioned earlier, Charles Colson wrote:

> The almost surrealistic style was so vivid that for all practical purposes it drowned out any biblical teaching. . . . The producers' goal was admirable—reaching out to young people raised on MTV—but if even a secular reviewer can sense a discrepancy between the biblical message and the style in which it is communicated, then surely we, too, must become more aware.[3]

Make no mistake about it: the *form* of Christian communication also can cancel out the *message!* Colson has rightly spoken. We preachers must become more aware of this.

Paul was aware. That's one of the reasons he refused to embrace a preaching philosophy that gave primary attention to exceptional oratorical prowess or a keen analysis of how the human mind works. Something else dominated his presentation that contrasted him from the secular public speakers of the day, especially those itinerant professors of wisdom for whom he actually had been mistaken at Athens (see Acts 17:18–22). He most certainly would have felt the same temptation in Corinth he had faced there, namely to employ a manner of speaking that might naturally seem to appeal more to the Greeks.

Winston Churchill, considered one of the most powerful orators in history, considered rhetoric to be his most valuable weapon. But biographer Norman Rose noted that he had a tendency to brandish it recklessly, employing artificial and extravagant language which was carefully designed to impress and to persuade. During his rise to fame as a politician, the twenty-three-year-old Churchill wrote:

> It is quite true. I do not care so much for the principles I advo-
> cate as for the impression which my words produce & the repu-
> tation they give me. This sounds [very] terrible . . . Perhaps to
> put it a little strongly, I should say that I [very] often yield to the
> temptation of adapting my facts to my phrases.[4]

But Rose's observation of Churchill's ability is even more frightening: "He possessed a [marvelous], though highly dangerous, gift: an innate ability to bewitch himself by the potency of his crafted, dazzling phrases."[5]

In recent years preachers have been encouraged to pattern their communication skills after newscasters, Hollywood actors, business leaders, and numerous other secular orators. The implication often is made that a failure to do so will result in an inability to communicate the gospel effectively to contemporary culture. Consequently, many preachers spend more time attending conferences and reading books on secular communications skills than they do immersing themselves in their message.

Because the preacher of the gospel never speaks on his own authority but solely on that of someone else, the apostle Paul refused to allow his manner of speech to *rise out above* his message. He completely denied the thought of ever depending upon the persuasive and argumentative resources of the public orators of his day, knowing that would have resulted only in glory for himself. Culture-driven preaching? No way! Purpose-driven preaching? Not a chance. Paul's preaching was driven by a passion for the glory of God, even if it meant being countercultural!

The Preacher in Preaching

Amidst all of the emphasis that is put on the abilities and talents of the preacher today, the New Testament paints quite a different picture. It describes gospel preachers as mere earthen vessels that contain a treasure (cf. 2 Cor. 4:7 ff.). The preacher is the earthen vessel; the treasure is the gospel as communicated through the Word of God. It seems that in many contexts today those two elements have been confused. Search committees develop profiles for pastoral candidates, and pastors pad their resumes to accommodate, all suggesting that the man is the treasure. And the little emphasis that is placed on his perspective and treatment of the Scriptures almost implies that the man's doctrine is nothing more than an earthen vessel. Contemporary preachers will have to adopt a different perspective of the preaching event and their role in it if they are to be effective.

The Awe of the Event

Students often ask me in preaching classes, "When do you get to the point that you don't get nervous when you preach?" I always answer them the same way. If the preacher ever gets to the point that he doesn't get a little nervous when he preaches, he better stop preaching because he's lost the awe of the task! To be sure, there's a certain amount of the jitters that disappear as a man gains experience and grows more confident in the preaching event. But he can never afford to lose his sense of awe and reverence for the high task of standing to speak for God.

Paul never lost his awe. He chose to respect the incredible responsibility God gave him to preach, so he used three expressions to describe his state during his tenure at Corinth—"weakness," "fear," and "much trembling" (1 Cor. 2:3). The three words are tied together by the initial verb in the sentence. These descriptions combine to underscore the reality that the preacher's personal giftedness, training, and experience are nothing but handicaps when they alone are put forth as the keys to impacting people's lives. Something different characterized Paul's approach.

A. T. Robertson described "with" (1 Cor. 2:3) as the "face-to-face preposition." When Paul came face-to-face with the people in Corinth who admired oratory and philosophic presentation, he was a poor and run-down figure indeed. His "weakness" may have been due to a number of factors—his unimpressive presence (cf. 2 Cor. 10:10), his shyness in venturing unaccompanied into strange territory (cf. Acts 17:15; 18:5), the moral depravation in the city of Corinth along with the potential hostility of the Jews (cf. Acts 18:5–6), a physical malady (cf. Gal. 4:13), or his "thorn in the flesh" (2 Cor. 12:7). He had been in jail in Philippi, he had been run out of Thessalonica and Berea on a rail, and he had politely bowed out of Athens. No doubt, all of these factors conglomerated to drain him of both physical and emotional strength.

But the construction in the language of the New Testament suggests that Paul's condition was not primarily due to some physical malady in his body. The language indicates a sense of weakness which determines one's conduct. It wasn't primarily his outward circumstances but his personal shortcomings that zapped the apostle's strength. So what was the resulting conduct? The text says that "fear" and "trembling" issued forth from Paul's weak condition. The apostle used these two words together in several other passages to refer to a deep concern over an important, urgent issue (cf. 2 Cor. 7:15; Eph. 6:5; Phil. 2:12). In Corinth, that issue was the need for the gospel to take root in an unfertile field. Paul was not fearful for his own life or for the possibility of presenting an ineffective gospel but for the possibility that the gospel would be rejected. And it made Paul feel weak when he thought that he might not be equal to the great responsibility to which he had been called.

How desperately we need such humility in preaching today! Oh, how we need preachers who will respect the responsibility like that! Preachers need the attitude described by the great H. A. Ironside:

> How often as one thinks of facing an audience, the heart fails and the spirit cries out, "O Lord, what can I do, what can I say? Suppose I should make a mistake, suppose I should give the wrong message, how dire the effect might be on some! I can never undo it for eternity!" I can see Paul bowing before God every time he contemplated going out to preach the Word, and crying out, "O Lord, keep me from mistakes, let me have just the right word, give me to be Thy messenger, save me from trying to attract attention to myself, save me from glorifying man."[6]

The responsibility of preaching ought to make a man weak. It ought to make him fear and tremble! He ought to revere it!

The Attitude in the Event

The way many churches go about searching for pastors and the way many preachers politic for positions makes one think that what is at stake is the future success of a *Fortune 500* company. What is at stake, however, is far more important than the prosperity of a major corporation. What is at stake is the glory of the God of the universe and the subsequent life change it effects in people who are exposed to it. That's why Paul approached his preaching with a little different attitude than did some of his colleagues in Corinth. Acknowledging the paramount task he had been assigned and the inability of human wisdom to tackle it, the apostle humbly depended upon the supernatural work of the Divine to change lives.

What Paul claimed in the current passage is that his work had not been done in his own strength but in humble dependence upon Christ's strength (cf. 2 Cor. 12:10). Although neither the Acts narrative nor his own writings leave us with the impression that Paul was a weak man, he spoke much about the claim (see 1 Cor. 4:10; 2 Cor. 11:30; 12:5, 9; Gal. 4:13). The arrogant Corinthians were being informed that even the great apostle could not do his work in Corinth from a spirit of self-sufficiency. He was humbly at the mercy of the power of the indwelling Christ.

Practically, the potency of this Christ life is manifested in direct proportion to the death of the preacher. John Piper points out that in the New Testament the cross of Christ is not only a past place of substitution for sin but a present place of execution of self-reliance and our love affair with the praise of man.[7] The biggest problem in Corinth with regard to preaching was pride, which always ended up in the preacher and the people getting the glory. The people were swept away with the presentations of men, aligning themselves with their preacher of choice. Paul critically observed that they professed, "'I am of Paul,' or 'I am of Apollos,' or 'I am of Cephas,' or 'I am of Christ'" (1 Cor. 1:12). The apostle's whole agenda here is to counter such an abdication of the glory of God "that no flesh should glory in His presence" (1 Cor. 1:29). He even prefaces his comments on preaching in our text under consideration by quoting from Jeremiah 9:24, "He who glories, let him glory in the LORD" (1 Cor. 1:31).

The crucified Christ beckons preachers to humility and selflessness in preaching. Are not the volleying for position and the quest to make a name for oneself two of the great monsters haunting the ministry today? Regarding Paul's message as stated in 1 Corinthians 2:2, Piper wrote:

> I think what he means is that he set his mind to be so saturated with the crucifying power of the cross that in everything he said and did, in all his preaching, there would be the aroma of death—death to self-reliance, death to pride, death to boasting in man. In this aroma of death the life that people would see would be the life of Christ, and the power that people would see would be the power of God.[8]

While many of us are trying to climb the ladder, Paul was championing the life of the cross. Preacher, if your preaching is constantly calling people's attention to the crucified life, then those of us who listen to you will not have time to sing your praises.

To say the least, the Corinthians weren't very impressed with Paul's personal presence (see 2 Cor. 10:10). And listeners today won't be either. Most preachers will face similar difficult conditions. It will be just preacher and people, and the time for talking will be past. The preacher will face people who are closed to the gospel, people who prefer a different style than we possess, and people who long for oratorical skill and worldly philosophy. Often they will face those conditions on the heels of bad experiences, physical weakness, financial restraints, and other elements that will weaken them. But, like Paul, preachers of the Word must redeem these occasions merely as pointed reminders that it's not about them. Such a spirit of humility paves the way for powerful proclamation of God's Word!

The Persuasion in Preaching

Recently one of my students told me about visiting a rapidly growing megachurch worship service in which the pastor delivered a suave sermon on sexual promiscuity. And he did it without hardly even mentioning the Bible! As he and a friend, who was a member of the church, were leaving, his friend asked him what he thought of the preacher's message. My student hesitantly responded that it was a helpful message, but that he wouldn't exactly call it "preaching." The shocked friend quickly came to the defense of his pastor and exclaimed, "Well, he must be doing it right or else all of these people wouldn't continue to come hear him!"

It appears that many contemporary approaches to preaching are evaluated based upon the number of people that respond. Such is just one of many expressions of the twenty-first-century church's worship of pragmatism—*If people respond, then it must be right!* But this shortsighted conclusion fails to recognize that there are many forms of persuasion in communication. And the validity of approaches to persuasion in preaching is not necessarily gauged on people's response but by each approach's consistency with the nature and purpose of the gospel. In fact, some presentations may even be moral and appealing but all the while be depending upon the wisdom of the world for their persuasive power!

Worldly Wisdom in Corinthian Speech

The bewildering thing about the Corinthian party spirit was that all parties seemed to profess the same gospel. At least one difference, however, was the various means by which different preachers apparently sought to persuade their listeners. But Paul was no party animal. In order to protect his preaching from worldly persuasion, he refused to embrace the alluring wisdom of the world in his content and presentation. He initially responded to the party problem by describing the very nature of the gospel and God's simple reason for giving it that nature. The nature of the gospel is foolishness to the world but salvation to those who would believe (see 1 Cor. 1:18–25). The reason for such a nature was so God alone would get the glory and not man (see 1 Cor. 1:26–31).

Paul's preaching lined up with both the nature and purpose of the gospel. After confessing his human weakness, he described what kind of preaching presentation *did not* line up with the gospel and, therefore, was not a part of his repertoire. The result of his humble reliance upon the indwelling Christ was not proclamation that was distinguished by "persuasive words of human wisdom" (1 Cor. 2:4). While Paul distinguishes between his "speech" and his "preaching," the former is likely a reference to content while the latter describes the actual public proclamation. He is referring here to both the message he preached and the way he preached it. Neither, according to the apostle, was characterized by man's manipulative presentation.

These words are a blatant denial of the cleverness of the first-century rhetorician who often couched his thoughts in flights of oratory and philosophy. "Persuasive" translates an extremely unusual word which means "enticing." It refers to words which are employed specifically with the intent of enticing listeners to respond. "Wisdom" clearly is a reference to worldly wisdom. Now don't be fooled, friend. The apostle Paul was a fan of persuasion (see Acts 13:43; 17:4–5; 18:4; 19:26; 28:24; 2 Cor. 5:11). But what Paul strongly opposed was the employment of persuasive words which were dictated by worldly wisdom. He knew that any and every form of human wisdom robs the gospel of its power.

Worldly Wisdom in Contemporary Sermons

Regardless of how impressive and persuasive it may be, man's efforts of coercion render God's work impotent to a certain degree. Contrary to some popular trends today, there is absolutely no place for planned theatrics and techniques to manipulate response. It is certainly possible for people to respond to an emotional appeal or highly charged presentation without possessing a true knowledge and conviction of God. The deceptive thing about this reality is that those kinds of approaches often result in a wider and more receptive hearing, but they often leave listeners in their same spiritual condition and no closer to Christ or His likeness.

One of the questions that I hear quite often when people in various churches find out that I teach preaching is, "How do you do that?" The question is sincere because they know that preaching is a calling of God. But they wonder how any man could possibly teach someone how to do the divine task. Without getting into a technical and academic discussion, I usually explain to them that preaching primarily involves the communication of God's Word. And there's nothing that any man can do to make God's Word more potent. It's already the most potent force in the universe. But there are things we can do to veil its potency. In other words, while the preacher can't learn to do things that will make him a more powerful preacher, he can do things that make him less prominent so that God's power is released in the preaching event. So then, I tell my curious friends that I prefer to look at teaching preaching as teaching guys what to do and not to do in order to stay out of the way of God's power.

One of the most deceptively subtle forms of human wisdom today is the amount of extrabiblical information that fills contemporary sermons. While it is certainly not wrong for a preacher to utilize information from outside the Bible to support, illustrate, or apply the truth of God's Word, a line is crossed when the observations and assertions of some other preacher, psychologist, researcher, or futurist become the primary content of sermons. And it doesn't matter whether the contentions are those of a Christian or non-Christian. If they are derived from some means other than the study of God's Word, they are still man's wisdom. While the wisdom of some people is better informed than that of others, all extrabiblical information is still just human wisdom. And regardless of how enticing it may be, human wisdom will never positively affect the spiritual makeup of mankind.

I am speaking here of the difference between addressing listeners, as Ironside said, on the "soul-plane" instead of the spiritual plane.[9] Preaching on the soul-plane involves information which simply appeals to the human mind. In this kind of preaching, the preacher can wrongly interpret how in a psychological moment he grabbed the audience with a tender story, practical principle, or "relevant" application. And by virtue of the people's response to an individual message or the growth of a church where such preaching is the norm, the preacher and people falsely and pragmatically conclude that the "soul-plane" preaching is to be credited. And yet it is possible that not one responder in the crowd has had their spirit reached or transformed.

Persuasive words of *human* wisdom always get in the way of God's power. They always depend on man's sufficiency and are manifested in man's presentation. And they always fail to provide listeners with any supernatural catalyst for life change. Worst of all, persuasive words of human wisdom always bring glory to the human instrument instead of to the God he professes to proclaim. It has been said that the great preacher Jonathan Edwards often read his sermons so that he would not be guilty of using human persuasive techniques to gain a response. He wanted to ensure that the results were authentically derived by supernatural means and that God got all the glory.

The Proof in Preaching

I recently read a book on preaching to postmoderns, which was released at the dawn of the new millennium. It contained a fairly thorough treatment of the nature of postmodern thinking and how preaching should be shaped accordingly. But I was absolutely blown away when I finished it without ever running across even one mention of the role of the Holy Spirit in the task. How do you discuss preaching in any context without giving serious consideration to the supernatural work of God's Spirit?

From beginning to end, preaching is the communication of the Holy Spirit. John Knox said, "True preaching from start to finish is the work of the Spirit."[10] The Holy Spirit inspired the Word of God that we preach. He illuminates our understanding to its meaning and anoints our communication of it. He enlightens the minds of listeners to the message, convicts their hearts, and prompts them to respond. Preaching is the Holy Spirit's deal! And as listeners come face-to-face with God's Word rightly preached, His power is proven in the supernatural work of His Spirit in their hearts and minds.

The Evidence of the Spirit

Paul's preaching gave evidence of spiritual power, and he resolved to show that supernatural power in his preaching. With his first mention of the Holy Spirit in this epistle, the apostle continues to wed the subject of preaching content to the necessary resource for powerful proclamation. Conforming his preaching to what he had been saying about the "foolishness" of the gospel, his naked presentation of this simple message convincingly demonstrated the power of God. And the unveiling of the power of God revealed the glory of God!

After revealing the kind of presentation he did not employ (see 1 Cor. 2:1), Paul here described the kind of presentation he *did* employ—one which evidenced the power of God and His Spirit (see 1 Cor. 2:4). The word "demonstration" is found nowhere else in the New Testament and signifies the most rigorous kind of proof about some claim or fact. Paul claimed that when he got in the face of the Corinthians, his human frailty combined with his familiar message of the crucified Christ gave evidence to the power of the Spirit in the most convincing way. God honored the combination of a crucified earthen vessel filled with His supernatural message!

The two prepositional phrases here—"of the Spirit" and "of power"—likely do not indicate that the proof to which Paul refers was offered by the Spirit and power. Instead, they support the idea that the proof was showing the presence of the Spirit and power in Paul's preaching. There can be no doubt that Paul has in mind here the miracles that God worked through Jesus, the apostles, and prophets which evidenced the truth of the proclamation of the gospel (eg., Acts 2:22, 43; Rom. 15:19; 2 Cor. 12:12; Heb. 2:4). At the same time, he was also cognizant of the passing of the apostolic office and the continued manifestation of the many gifts of the Spirit, some of which involved Spirit-empowered proclamation right there in Corinth (see chapters 12 and 14). Paul's treatise on the superiority of prophecy over tongues and his prediction of the result right there in Corinth is an indication that the apostle did not limit the evidence of supernatural power to miraculous signs (see 1 Cor. 14:20–25).

The Encouragement of the Spirit

The construction in our passage also reveals two assurances that provide great encouragement for the preacher. First, there is no spiritual power apart from the Holy Spirit. The two words—"Spirit" and "power"—form a kind of unit, indicating that they refer to the same thing. Second, there is no preaching of God's Word apart from spiritual power. Don't forget that this unit is still qualifying "speech" and "preaching" at the beginning of the verse. The content and presentation of the gospel are never without the accompaniment of the supernatural power of God's Holy Spirit! When the preacher relies on these two assurances, his presentation is sure to be infused with the mighty hand of God! The result will be that the certainty of scriptural truth for the believer will be as complete and as objective as the certainty of scientific truth for the secular mind. Divine power will grip pliable hearts and drive them to salvation and Christlikeness.

We ought to get real nervous today when little distinction is made between the nature of Christian preaching and other forms of public speaking. In keeping with the trend to lead the church according to the same *modus operandi* as successful corporations, many preachers today seem to be dancing to the music of the pied piper of secular oratory. How could something that is naturally initiated and operated be allowed to determine the success of something that is supernaturally sanctioned, anointed, and presented?

Success in ministry is not dependent upon the preacher's ability to clothe his preaching in rhetorical excess. What he needs is for God to get involved and wrap his human weakness in His spiritual power. While Jesus was deity clothed in humanity, in the preaching event preachers must be humanity clothed in deity! The only thing they can depend upon to make their preaching effective is the work of the Spirit as He manifests His power through the preacher's human weakness. That includes all of his weaknesses, all of his bad experiences, all of his tainted backgrounds, all of his big mistakes—everything! That's when God gets all the glory.

Where Do I Go from Here . . .

Now that you have considered Paul's approach to preaching regarding the *content* and the *resource,* you may proceed one of two ways as indicated by the shaded areas on the chart below. The (▼) symbol indicates the thematic development of the remainder of his preaching philosophy as revealed in 1 Corinthians 2:1–5. If you have chosen this path, proceed to chapter 3, "The Motive in Preaching." The (➡) symbol indicates the continued development of the *resource* from philosophical and then practical standpoints. If you are following this path, proceed to chapter 5, "The Shepherd's Power." If you have not yet read the introduction to part 2, "Passion-Driven Shepherdology," be sure to do that first.

Table 2.1

	PART 1 (Biblical)		PART 2 (Philosophical)		PART 3 (Practical)
(Content)	Chapter 1: The Message of Preaching ▼	➡	Chapter 4: The Shepherd's Stewardship ▼	➡	Chapter 7: Preaching as Worship ▼
(Resource)	Chapter 2: The Means for Preaching ▼	➡	Chapter 5: The Shepherd's Power ▼	➡	Chapter 8: Preaching with Potency ▼
(Goal)	Chapter 3: The Motive in Preaching	➡	Chapter 6: The Shepherd's Relevance	➡	Chapter 9: Preaching for Eternity

*"That your faith should not be in the wisdom of men
but in the power of God."*
1 Corinthians 2:5

CHAPTER 3

The Motive in Preaching:

GOD'S PURPOSE VS. MAN'S PRAGMATISM

A casual perusal of the religion page in most newspapers says much about the state of preaching today. The sermon titles remind us that we live in an ecclesiastical age of shallow clichés, warm and fuzzy fix-its, and easy pragmatism: "How to Have a Happy Marriage"; "How to Raise Teenagers"; "How to Manage Your Money"; "How to Develop Healthy Relationships"; "How to Deal with Stress in the Workplace." Even if they're couched in other terminology, the number of how-to sermons being advertised, delivered, and consumed any given week is quite astounding. Many contemporary preachers are spitting out pragmatic fix-it messages like they can fix just about anything.

Paul refused to stoop to such pragmatism in his preaching. He instead aimed high, determined by the very purpose of God in Christ. In the last phrase of this first paragraph in 1 Corinthians 2, he addressed the motive of preaching in a clear purpose clause indicated by the word *that* (1 Cor. 2:5). Although it is directly tied to the preceding verse, the purpose statement actually encompasses the preceding four verses as well as the thoughts at the end of the previous chapter. Everything Paul did in his preaching ministry was so that it might line up with the agenda of the ages—*the glory of God* (cf. 1 Cor. 1:26–31)!

The Preacher's Target

Can I be transparent for a moment? Personally, I don't think I'm smart enough to address most of those subjects mentioned above. Sure I can attach some Bible verses and scriptural principles to most any subject, but when I reflect on the "practical" steps and principles being offered by many preachers and consumed by many congregants today, I simply don't have enough experience, expertise, or even biblical material to address most of those topics! Nor do I have the time to spend shoring up in every area of life in order to address them with some semblance of authority. And I'm not about to stand in front of my church and say, "Now here's how you raise your teenagers," when I'm scrambling to figure out how to raise my own!

Someone has said that if you shoot at nothing, you'll always hit it! While preachers can't afford to aim at nothing, neither can they afford to aim at an unrealistic target. Trying to provide pragmatic solutions to all of life's problems and attempting to offer pat answers to all of life's questions is incredibly unrealistic! Thus, Paul was very clear about what the preacher is to be aiming at— authentic faith in the lives of listeners.

The Faith of the Believer

Paul was focused on that one target in his sermons, and that target reflected the purpose of God in preaching. Some Bible scholars believe that the presence of the definite article with "faith" indicates that Paul is here referring to the substance of the Corinthians' belief based on the person and work of Christ. In other words, "your faith" would be the body of Christian doctrine that they embraced, the content of the gospel in its most complete form. Such an understanding would be equivalent to "the faith which was once for all delivered to the saints" (Jude 3), for which we are to contend. As with "the testimony of God" in the first verse, this understanding of "faith" is equivalent today to the content of God's revealed and recorded Word, the Bible.

The New Testament usage of "your faith" followed by the possessive preposition (i.e., "of you"), however, does not support such an interpretation. The "faith" to which Paul refers in this purpose clause is the simple act of belief with the predominant idea of trust. Closely akin to the New Testament word for *persuade*, it speaks of firm persuasion or conviction based upon hearing. And it's always used of faith in God or Christ or some other spiritual thing. Paul was anxious to build believers' trust in God and His power, not in people. He knew that was the only faith that would last and the only way God's work would be accomplished in their lives.

Building the listener's faith is a subject that gets little attention in contemporary preaching. Like so many other aspects of the spiritual side of preaching, it is so hard to measure. And if we can't measure it, we usually don't talk about it. But the heart response offered by those who listen to sermons is going to be lashed to something. And that something is determined by the content of the sermon. It is truly a sad day when pastors make converts to themselves because they call their congregants to a misplaced faith by virtue of the substance of their preaching. To be sure, authentic faith is birthed as a result of right content, preaching the very Word of God (cf. Rom. 10:17).

This goal of building authentic faith was also a counter to the "wisdom of men" that Paul despised. From the beginning of his ministry in Corinth, he desired to ground his converts in the right kind of faith and to make them independent of human wisdom. That's why he refused to employ techniques of coercion, excessive rhetorical arts, and subject matter that was palatable to secular interests. Instead, he concentrated on the simple message which was so unpalatable to natural men—the message of the cross.

The Faith of the Body

The faith of individual believers ultimately became the hub around which the community of faith was formed. Thus, the two kinds of "faith" mentioned above—trust and doctrine—actually are not mutually exclusive. As the Word of God gives birth to genuine and lasting faith, that faith in turn fleshes out the body of belief that is paramount for the life and health of the faith community. For Paul the two kinds of faith were inseparable (see Rom. 10:1–17; 1 Cor. 15:1–19). Right doctrine births real faith, and real faith shapes right doctrine. In essence, it's a continual cycle. At the same time the cycle can become perverted. Wrong doctrine gives birth to false and failing faith, and false and failing faith leads to belief in a wrong doctrine. Paul knew that the totality of what his listeners believed about God in Christ had to be rooted in God's Word.

In Ephesians, Paul clearly pointed out that the very unity of the church regarding this body of belief was the initial goal of the pastor's spiritual equipping (see Eph. 4:11–13). The relationship between the body of Christian doctrine and unity is clear in the Letter to the Ephesians: faith is the axis around which the church's unity revolves. He had already pleaded with them to endeavor "to keep the unity of the Spirit in the bond of peace" (Eph. 4:3; see also 1 Cor. 1:10). This exhortation was obviously based upon the believers' calling to oneness in the Prince of Peace, Jesus Christ (see Eph. 2:14–18; 4:1). Paul knew that the lack of faithful teaching of God's Word, the absence of careful examination of traditions, the influences of the world, and the natural inclinations toward carnality would all slice the church's doctrine into many varying and even contradictory fragments.

The Corinthian congregation was a classic, living example of how disunity in the church comes from doctrinal ignorance and spiritual immaturity. In fact, Paul had already stated that his solution to their disunity was for everyone to hold the same understandings and opinions and to speak the same truths (see 1 Cor. 1:10). So Paul's preaching purpose—the thing at which he aimed—was such a belief on the part of individual Corinthians that would become the very substance of their corporate existence. Whether or not they would have "faith" was not the issue. Paul knew they would embrace something; everybody does. But he wanted to make sure their belief system was formed on the right foundation. This faith would function as the supernatural glue that would hold them together as the body of Christ. There will never be unity in any church apart from doctrinal integrity.

I may not be smart enough to address all the perceived needs and relevant subjects with just the right fix-it sermons. But what I can do is simply be faithful to preach the Bible and its Christ, believing that God will produce a faith in His people that will bind them together in community. And when people embrace the genuine faith of Scripture and walk with God accordingly, it will take care of all that stuff that needs fixing. It may sound simplistic, but it's really not. Walking with God by faith and living with others in faith community can be complicated stuff, and it's a lot more challenging than just fixing your marriage or raising your kids!

The Preacher's Take-away

Alex Haley, the author of *Roots,* had a picture in his office showing a turtle sitting on top of a fence. The picture was there to remind him of a lesson he learned earlier in his life: "If you see a turtle on a fence post, you know he had some help." About the lesson Haley said, "Any time I start thinking, 'Wow, isn't this marvelous what I've done!' I look at that picture and remember how this turtle—me—got up on that post." Paul defined preaching in terms of a "turtle on the fence." When people see a turtle on the fence, they begin to focus on the one who put him there. When Paul preached, he wanted the faith with which people responded to be shackled to the power of God in Christ. That means He gets the glory!

This drives us back to an age-old question in preaching—*What should listeners walk away with?* To say it another way, *What is the sermon's take-away?* Preachers and congregations will do well to embrace and apply Paul's answer to those questions.

Power of God

Should the preacher even be desiring that listeners draw from his sermons pat answers for all of their questions and needs? Paul seems to suggest not. The phrase "be in" (1 Cor. 2:5) technically means "to rest upon." Paul wanted his listeners to walk away from his sermons embracing a faith that was completely at home with and dependent upon "the power of God" (1 Cor. 2:5). That is the primary take-away toward which all preaching should move.

Paul could have countered his reference to man's "wisdom" with a contrasting reference to God's "wisdom." But instead he chose to refer to God's "power." He earlier had defined the power of God as the "message of the cross" (1 Cor. 1:18) and even "Christ" Himself (1 Cor. 1:24), whom he also described as the "wisdom of God." The message of the crucified Christ as revealed in Scripture is potent with supernatural power to change lives! Unlike the intellectual nature of man's wisdom, every word of the gospel is real and powerful. And "this power of changeless grace is to be the basis of our faith."[1]

Listen, friend! This is huge in light of the affinity in our day for psychological preaching. The gospel was never intended to be just good advice for me, telling me how to navigate daily life. Nor is it simply a message *about* God's power. It *is* God's power! Paul told the Romans that he was "not ashamed of the gospel of Christ, for it is the power of God to salvation for everyone who believes, for the Jew first and also for the Greek" (Rom. 1:16). Today it seems that many preachers not only don't believe it is the power of God; they appear to be ashamed of it. The gospel is veiled beyond the point of recognition with extrabiblical material that supposedly makes the sermon relevant and interesting. More and more messages talk *about* the power of God but never contain enough Bible to actually expose people to the potency of the gospel.

Pastoral Guidance

Most people would agree that one of the worst things a counselor can do when counseling with individuals is to preach to them. Now by that I'm not referring to the need to offer biblical counsel or to challenge people to align their conduct with biblical norms. Certainly those would be appropriate. But I'm speaking of the development of biblical texts and the passionate exhortation to adhere to them that are characteristic to corporate proclamation. Such efforts would be overwhelming and, therefore, out of place in most private counseling situations. Private counseling and public proclamation are two distinct ministries. While there is certainly some overlap between the two, they are largely different ministries with different purposes. And, therefore, they normally are conducted in different ways.

Tragically, and equally incongruous, many preachers today go into the pulpit and attempt to conduct large-group counseling. This has been the predominant trend in preaching since the early part of the last century when pastoral preaching took a radically different turn. Historically, one of the major functions of the sermon had been to provide pastoral instruction to guide the *congregation* in living the Christ life. But for various reasons, the role of the sermon in pastoral preaching began to shift from a focus on corporate Christian living to instruction and care for the *individual*.[2]

This radical change in the preaching event has contributed to the development of a new meaning for the term *pastoral*. Rather than men who guide congregations by preaching and teaching the crucified life, it has taken on the connotation of support, acceptance, care, affirmation, healing, and even unconditional positive regard given to individuals. Thomas Long noted that the image of preacher as pastor

> almost inevitably views the hearers of sermons as a collection of
> discrete individuals who have personal problems and needs
> rather than as a group, a community, a church with a mission.
> The public, corporate, and systemic dimensions of the gospel
> are often downplayed in favor of more personalistic themes.[3]

Consequently, pastoral guidance and even pastoral preaching are now regarded as individualized care given by the shepherd to *individual sheep* as opposed to the historical emphasis on shepherds who feed and lead a *flock*.[4] The needs of the sheep are now categorized with problems of the individual and family like relationships, loneliness, conflict, midlife crisis, happiness, and self-esteem. So in the sermon the preacher simply identifies a problem and offers a solution.

The modern emphasis in the pulpit on the individual listeners and their personal life issues can be traced to a significant degree to the preaching of Harry Emerson Fosdick. His popular pulpit ministry became a model for many pastors during the first part of the twentieth century. Fosdick admittedly began with the questions of people in his congregation and then tried to find answers from Scripture, attempting to "throw such light on it from the spirit of Christ."[5] His focus was so much on individuals and their problems that he actually believed the effectiveness of the sermon should be measured by the number of people who wanted to see the preacher for personal counseling as a result!

The modern incarnation of this philosophy is manifested in the contemporary enthrallment with "felt needs" preaching. The listeners in our therapeutic age love it because of its perceived "relevant" quality and its focus upon their needs. This problem-solving preaching moves from a vexing personal problem to a psychologically sound "Christian" answer. But the undetected problem is that its "problem orientation" leans toward only comforting truths.[6]

James Thompson rightly summarizes the breakdown of this personal and medicinal view of pastoral preaching. First, it owes more to modern therapeutic understanding than to the roots of its image in the life of a shepherd. The shepherd's task was not only to comfort and support but also to guide, protect, and ensure the general welfare of those in his charge. Second, its emphasis on acceptance neither confronts the listeners with a word of judgment nor offers guidance on the concrete demands of the Christ life. Third, it is understood in almost exclusively individualistic terms with the focus on how "I" can get something. Fourth, it has difficulty distinguishing between the legitimate needs of the listeners and the wants that have been created in our own society.[7]

Listen, friend! The cross of Jesus Christ with the demands it makes on our daily lives is the very wisdom and power of God. To be sure, it will bring comfort to the hurting heart. But it will be a lasting comfort because it grows out of the crucified life. The Jesus Christ that is revealed from Genesis to Revelation in the Scripture is both the power of God and the wisdom of God (see 1 Cor. 1:24). That's what most of these first two chapters in 1 Corinthians are about—a contrast between God's wisdom and power with that of the world!

Perpetual Growth

Like the ongoing application of the crucified Christ, this discussion of faith need not be limited to the salvation of sinners. Certainly the "wisdom of God" included the knowledge that the cross was the only way to salvation. And we can be sure that the "power of God" spoke of the supernatural dynamic that the cross provides in actually saving someone. But both the wisdom of God and the power of God continue to be relevant and effectual for the perpetual growth of the believer.

This is evident as the apostle Paul goes on to say that "you are in Christ Jesus, who became for us wisdom from God—and righteousness and sanctification and redemption" (1 Cor. 1:30). Believers are not only saved by God's wisdom, but they are given God's wisdom on an ongoing basis (cf. Eph. 1:17–18; 2 Pet. 3:18). As Christians, we also receive God's righteousness. Not only are we made right with God, but we participate in His righteousness (cf. Rom. 4:5; 2 Cor. 5:21; Phil. 3:9). And we also receive God's sanctification. We are declared righteous in Christ upon salvation, but we are made holy in Christ through the process of sanctification (cf. Eph. 2:10; Rom. 8:4–11; 2 Cor. 3:18; Gal. 5:22–23). Finally, believers receive God's redemption, and Christ is given to us as "the guarantee of our inheritance until the redemption of the purchased possession" (Eph. 1:14).

Do you see the implications for preaching? Paul later said that he intentionally preached nothing but Jesus Christ crucified (see 1 Cor. 2:2), because in Him the listener had all he or she needed—wisdom, righteousness, sanctification, and redemption. Consequently, the call here is for contemporary preachers to faithfully preach the Scriptures as weekly fare to their congregations, the very Scriptures that speak of the crucified Christ from Genesis to Revelation. The more people get to know this Christ, the more of His wisdom, righteousness, and sanctification and redemption they have to navigate through daily life. And I would much rather have the source of those treasures nurtured in my life than I would have some preacher randomly apply a small segment of one of them to some felt need in my life!

Influenced by their Greek culture that longed for the latter, the Corinthians apparently gravitated toward the world's substitutes. And so blow the winds of both the pulpit and pew in our day. To the secular mind, the cross will always appear to be nothing more than utter nonsense. But the cross on which Jesus hung for all people proved to be God's real wisdom and real power. The world's wisdom will never lead people to God, nor will it give them supernatural power over the evil and temptation that plague them. But the preacher and congregation who determine to offer contemporary listeners the real thing will find themselves as trout swimming upstream.

So what's the take-away in the sermons delivered in your local church? Do the people who listen to them see a turtle on a fence, or do they just see a turtle? What do they really believe in? Is it the pastor? Some human agenda or lesser religious cause? Or is it the body of doctrine in which God is shown to have done all the work through the crucified Christ to redeem them. Preaching that magnifies pragmatism is preaching that will ultimately produce a confidence in a preacher or his philosophy. And people will eat it up. On the other hand, preaching that employs practical application as it exalts only the crucified Christ is preaching that will produce a faith wholly and totally in the power of God. The latter is a strong, active faith because its object is the One who put the turtle on the fence. Then God gets the glory!

The Preacher's Temptation

I finally found a diet I like. It allows me to eat all the meat and fatty stuff I want. The downside? No carbohydrates and no sugar. Although I certainly enjoy bread and pasta, I'm not really a big sweets eater. But I love meat. I would rather have two helpings of meat than a dessert any day! So the trade-offs with this diet are more appealing to me than any other that I've found. And the incredible thing is that it actually works! If I'm faithful to the plan, I can really control my weight while still eating extra portions of some of the things I love the most. The way it works is simple. Our bodies store carbohydrates, sugars, fats, proteins, and the like. To get energy the body will burn carbohydrates and sugars first. That's why high-carb and high-sugar items are consumed by athletes for quick energy. So you simply starve the body of carbs and sugars, and then it's forced to burn the fat in your body.

Did I mention being "faithful" to the plan? What I've discovered is that when I cheat, my body gets new doses of carbs and sugars along with the fats and proteins, and it goes back to burning them in the normal order. Essentially, when the body gets these mixed messages, the carbs and sugars cancel out the proteins and fats. Then the fat stays, and the diet loses its punch! Paul knew that when the gospel was mixed with anything else, its power would be canceled out. He knew what preachers today better realize—listeners will always "eat up" the carbs and sugars of worldly wisdom before they consume the meat of the gospel! In our attempt to be real and relevant, we will always face the temptation to mix biblical truth with the wisdom of the world.

The Description of Mixed Messages

Like so many congregations today, the Corinthians apparently had grown accustomed to preaching that sent mixed signals. The construction in the language of the New Testament seems to call specific attention to "the wisdom of men." Paul seemed to be making a point of separating the phrase off in order to draw a striking contrast between man's wisdom and the preferred substance of their faith. The church at Corinth was placing too much emphasis on the thoughts and ideas of men. Apparently, some Corinthian believers had developed an affinity for preaching that featured the rhetorical devices and even secular philosophies of the day.

If we back up a little, we find a hint of the apparent problem in Corinth when it came to preaching and listening to preaching. Do you remember the party animal mentality as everybody was aligning themselves with their favorite preacher (see 1 Cor. 1:12)? Following that mild rebuke, the apostle seems to draw a distinction between his preaching and that which at least some of those preachers had begun to practice. He said God had called him "to preach the gospel, *not with wisdom of words,* lest the cross of Christ should be made of no effect" (1 Cor. 1:17; emphasis added). In the language of the New Testament, the phrase "wisdom of words" is more literally translated as something like "wisdom-statement," indicating some accepted expression of worldly philosophy. Evidently, the Corinthians had begun to gravitate toward a kind of preaching that synthesized the wisdom of the world with the gospel of Christ, a kind of preaching that was especially persuasive. And Paul deemed it harmful to the contents of the gospel because it made it "of no effect" (1 Cor. 1:17; cf. also 2:1, 5).

Now don't misunderstand. The Corinthians had not denied the gospel or ceased to preach the cross of Christ. They simply had wed it with the wisdom of the world to the point that the gospel took a backseat. F. W. Grosheide explains:

> The Corinthians had not come to the point where they no
> longer believed in the atoning work of Christ, but they never-
> theless attached themselves in such a measure to the wisdom of
> the world that Paul is constrained to speak of a *making void* of
> the *cross of Christ.* The apostle does not say that the
> Corinthians had made void the cross of Christ, nor does he
> associate his warning with one of the "parties" of 12. He simply
> states that he has not preached the gospel to the Corinthians
> with such wisdom as they desired, lest the cross of Christ should
> *be made void.*[8]

The time-honored ideas and assertions of respected personalities proved detrimental by capturing the attention of the hearers and preventing the gospel from coming to its full rights.

Let me give you a biblical example and then a contemporary application of this. The Judaizers in Galatia had embraced a similar kind of synthetic gospel that rendered the true gospel powerless. They mingled the gospel with the law, thereby nullifying the former. Their "wisdom-statement" was a *law-Christ,* a Christ which does not exist. In Corinth it was a *wisdom-gospel* or *philosophy-gospel,* a gospel meshed with the proud and prevailing Greek philosophic notions of the day. And the Corinthian believers apparently not only respected it; they screamed to have it preached to them. Why? Because it was "relevant" and "fresh"!

Today, the modern pulpit and congregation are plagued with a plethora of such strange bedfellows. From the *psychology-gospel* that produces so-called "life application" preaching to the *corporate-gospel* that impresses secular business and leadership principles upon the church, congregations everywhere are eating it up under the guise of relevant, contemporary preaching. And preachers are accommodating, making every effort to put the gospel (or what they perceive of it!) into what they deem to be a necessary and fitting form to connect with today's listeners.

Although many claim that such preaching is the same old gospel in a different package, they don't realize that listeners consume the carbs and sugars first, and frequently they never get to the protein of the meat. R. C. H. Lenski wrote:

> The combination of human wisdom with the gospel makes the gospel itself of none effect, . . . "empty," without inner reality or substance. The gospel would not only lose some quality or some part of itself; it would evaporate entirely and leave only a hollow show of gospel terms and phrases.[9]

The very fact that the 'wisdom-statement' seems to overshadow the gospel in almost every case is a pointed reminder that the pure gospel of Christ cannot be accommodated to the wisdom of the world.

Oftentimes such wisdom-statements are packaged today in so-called practical application. Contemporary preachers are being told that if they are to be true biblical and gospel preachers, they must give their listeners specific, practical instructions for applying the eternal truths of the text. But in order to offer such practical advice, they find themselves drawing from extrabiblical sources that address practical living. And what ends up happening in many cases is that the wisdom of men gets preached as eternal truth, often at the expense of the Word of God. While most of these preachers would profess to be conservative in their theology, they unknowingly have succumbed to the temptation of a very liberal homiletic by preaching as truth the wisdom of men instead of God's wisdom.

The Dangers of Mixed Messages

Mixing the message of the Bible with the wisdom of the world presents several dangers for both preachers and listeners. First, such conglomerations are hard to detect. They sometimes go unnoticed even by the preacher himself as well as by those who listen to his sermons. By all the standards we measure success in the church today—budgets, baptisms, buildings—preaching wisdom-statements appears to be effective. People flock to it because of its perceived relevant nature just like they did in Corinth. And as long as we allow tangible results to outweigh the faith which is rooted in the cross of Christ, the contemporary church will continue to be deceived by watered-down preaching.

Paul was not saying that the contemporary preacher should strive to make his words boring and bland. As long as the medium doesn't *rise out above* the message, preachers should take great measures to make the presentation of God's message creative and arresting. But the gospel must be presented in a clear, plain, and undiluted manner. And Paul knew that any dependence on the world's fodder or form certainly would water down the potent message of the crucified Christ.

Another danger of mixed sermons is their addictive nature. Paul knew that preaching dependent upon human logic and rhetoric for its impact would result in a faith that required the same elements to prop it up. Someone has said that the way you get people into church is the way you're going to have to keep them. The pastor who draws people by sermons filled with human philosophy and enticing rhetoric will have to continue in the same if he wishes to keep them coming back. But what will be the end of the faith of those members of some contemporary churches who have been nurtured under the preaching of worldly wisdom? Only time will tell.

A third danger with mixing the gospel with the world's wisdom is the possibility of misplaced faith. All too often people make willful decisions based upon the persuasive nature of sermons that simply stir their emotions or address personal needs. Sometimes it's because the discourse actually makes them feel like they need to do something about the subject at hand. Other times it's because they have a strong admiration and respect for the preacher. But when the emotions have waned or the preacher goes to another church, they find themselves questioning the truth of the matter. They wonder whether or not it was ever real. But when people place their faith in the power of God as revealed in Jesus Christ through the Scriptures, wavering feelings don't matter. Their faith lasts because it is rooted in God's sure testimony!

One other danger needs to be noted regarding the mixing of wisdom-statements with biblical truth. It presents truth as being in flux. The plural "men" (1 Cor. 2:5) used to describe the sources and dispensers of this human wisdom is significant. Paul was talking about *many* men from successive generations. The wisdom that comes from humanity is never constant, but it is ever-changing from age to age. Each new generation finds all kinds of unreality, untruth, and falsehoods in the worldly wisdom of the preceding generations. The classic illustration of this in our day is postmodernism, which is hailed as a total reaction to modernism. The generations that make up this age supposedly reject all things rational, logical, and scientific, the very values that many previous generations held as true. The individual resumes of the boomers, busters, X-ers, and millennials also represent the shifting sand of generational wisdom. And truth that is in flux is not truth on which authentic faith can be built.

The Devastation of Mixed Messages

The tragedy of people joining their faith to such uncertainty, however, runs deeper and more personal than any of these dangers. Mixed messages ultimately lead to the devastation of shipwrecked faith (cf. 1 Tim. 1:18–19). The wisdom of men—even Christian men—is that which has been gleaned from sources other than God's Word. It may come from completely random personal opinion or well-founded research. It may come by way of personal experience or through observation of the experiences of others. It may be a new discovery or information that has been passed down through the ages. But because it is man's wisdom, it will always be relative and subjective, making it an inadequate bedfellow for genuine faith.

In the introduction to this book, I referenced my personal struggle with the elusive "right way" to raise teenagers. I mentioned the radical differences between my two sons—contrasting temperaments, different ages, individual personalities, varying interests, unique life situations. The variables are infinite. But suppose I go to church needing some help on the subject and my well-meaning pastor preaches a sermon on "How to Raise Teenagers." In the message, he offers some general principles like bringing your children up in the nurture and admonition of the Lord, training up a child in the way he should go, and so forth. To "flesh out" the general principles, however, my sincere shepherd offers ten practical principles for raising my kids that were gleaned from the research and observation of a well-known Christian psychologist. In my desperation for parental help, I embrace *all* of my pastor's words as "the Word of God." And then I go home to apply my newfound faith.

You know what happens. The general biblical principles are objective and eternal. They always work. But the practical extrabiblical principles are subjective and relative at best. When applied uniformly to my radically different sons, I begin to discover inconsistencies and even failures. Maybe not at first, but sooner or later the infinite amount of ever-changing variables give rise to them. And guess who gets the blame. My pastor? No! The Christian psychologist? His name wasn't even mentioned. God gets the blame because the eternal truths and the relative truths were all presented as "thus saith the Lord." My faith buckles at the knees and maybe even falls. My faith has been joined with the wisdom of men, which always fizzles out. God gets the blame, and He certainly doesn't get the glory.

But what about information that might just be considered *universal* truth? Is there a place in preaching for proclaiming generally accepted principles that might be found outside the Bible? To be sure, all truth is God's truth. But God has not chosen to put His name on all truth in the way that He has done with the Holy Scriptures. Nor has He ordained all truth as that which defines, informs, or results from the gospel as delineated in the Bible. When people are given information—even extrabiblical truth—they are given the opportunity to place their faith in it, especially when it is offered by a preacher and presented in the context of "the Word of God." When they do embrace it, they end up putting their faith in something that is not supernatural, not inerrant, not infallible, not powerful, not eternal, and therefore not worth building their lives upon.

Besides, how does man determine something is actually and always true outside of the Word of God? Throughout history there have been many perceived "facts" that have been accepted as true only later to be discovered as false. At one time the world was believed to be flat. Gravity is a reality—until you go to the moon. As evangelical Christians, most of us have championed truth as being absolute, not relative. Reality is, however, that we can only be absolutely certain that *biblical* truth is absolute. The jury may still be out on a whole lot of extrabiblical truth. So why not stick with the stuff we know for sure? God is eternal. Jesus Christ is the same yesterday, today, and forever. The gospel is the power of God for salvation. All Scripture is inspired and, therefore, inerrant and infallible. Consequently, the material contained in the Bible is stuff people can trust not to change!

So what kind of diet is your congregation on? Is the meat of the gospel keeping listeners plugged in to the power of God in the life of the crucified Christ? Or are they being cheated as the carbs and sugars of wisdom-statements nullify their strength? Dear preacher, preach for spiritual health, not for practical help! And dear listener, hunger and thirst for an authentic faith, not a quick fix!

Where Do I Go from Here . . .

Now that you have completed a consideration of Paul's approach to preaching, you may proceed one of two ways as indicated by the shaded areas on the chart on the following page. If you desire to continue with the thematic development of the book, proceed to the introduction to part 2, "Passion-Driven Shepherdology," and then to chapter 4, "The Shepherd's Stewardship." The (➡) symbol indicates the development of the *goal* in preaching from philosophical and then practical standpoints. If you choose this path, proceed to chapter 6, "The Shepherd's Relevance." If you follow this route, be sure to first read the introduction to part 2, "Passion-Driven Shepherdology," if you have not already done so.

Table 3.1

	PART 1 (Biblical)		PART 2 (Philosophical)		PART 3 (Practical)
(Content)	Chapter 1: The Message of Preaching ▼	➡	Chapter 4: The Shepherd's Stewardship ▼	➡	Chapter 7: Preaching as Worship ▼
(Resource)	Chapter 2: The Means for Preaching ▼	➡	Chapter 5: The Shepherd's Power ▼	➡	Chapter 8: Preaching with Potency ▼
(Goal)	Chapter 3: The Motive in Preaching	➡	Chapter 6: The Shepherd's Relevance	➡	Chapter 9: Preaching for Eternity

Part 2

PASSION-DRIVEN SHEPHERDOLOGY

I planted a church during my master's work and ended up pastoring it for almost nine years. With all of their unique challenges, church starts usually afford some privileges and blessings that do not necessarily come with established congregations. Nobody ever said to me, "Well, sonny, we were here before you got here, and we'll be here when you leave." Nobody was there before me—my wife and I had started the work with just one other couple! We never heard anyone say, "We've never done it that way before." We had never done it *any* way before!

To be sure, I made a plethora of mistakes in pastoring that young congregation. I have often said that if I had it to do over again, I would do a million things differently. But amidst all of the faux pas, we stumbled across a few things by accident that proved to be productive. One of our good calls was leading our congregation to share in ministry, partly so that their pastor could give concentrated and protected time to the study and preaching of God's Word (see Acts 6:1–7). Consequently, from the outset of that ministry the first half of every one of my weekdays was given to sermon preparation through Bible study and prayer. And our congregation went to great pains to respect and protect that time.

On one particular morning I decided to break my sacred routine and make a hospital visit. A close friend and leader in our church was having surgery, and I thought I would just pop in and have prayer with the family. When I walked through the door of the waiting room, I was pleased to see the family accompanied by the man's Sunday School teacher, department and division directors, and one of our deacons. But my joy quickly turned to anxiousness as I watched the deacon get up and move aggressively toward me wearing a very stern countenance. When we met in the middle of the waiting room, he got right up in my face and said, "What are you doing here?" My first thought was, *Well, I'm the pastor, and pastors do things like this.* But before I could respond, he continued. "We've got plenty of people to handle things here," he said. "You're supposed to be in your study praying and preparing to bring us the Word of God on Sunday!" On that day, a hospital waiting room was transformed into a little corner of heaven for me.

Now I realize that there is more to pastoring than preaching, but a diligent investigation of pastoral work in the Bible reveals that the role has changed quite a bit. In the language of the New Testament the word *pastor* comes from the word *poimēn,* or *shepherd.* The term obviously emphasizes the pastoral role of caring and feeding. The shepherd is accompanied by two other New Testament pictures of the pastor. The word *elder* is the Greek word *presbuteros,* from which comes the word *presbyterian.* The word refers to mature age or character. The word *bishop* is the Greek word *episkopos,* from which comes the word *episcopal.* This word means "overseer" or "guardian" and refers to what a man does. All three terms—*shepherd, elder,* and *bishop*—are used of the same church leaders. While all three terms emphasize the pastoral role of caring and feeding, the term *shepherd* is the primary analogy in Scripture for the pastoral office, and it permeates the Old and New Testament teaching regarding the leadership of God's people.

Whatever this idea may mean for us today, the biblical picture is clear that the primary responsibility of the shepherd certainly is not to pet the sheep! Charles Jefferson was just one voice that arose throughout history to champion such an emphasis. While admitting that the job certainly involved elements of administration and remedial care, he asserted:

> That the feeding of the sheep is an essential duty of the shepherd-calling is known even to those who are least familiar with shepherds and their work. Sheep cannot feed themselves, nor water themselves. They must be conducted to the water and the pasture. . . . Everything depends on the proper feeding of the sheep. Unless wisely fed they become emaciated and sick, and the wealth invested in them is squandered. . . . When the minister goes into the pulpit, he is the shepherd in the act of feeding.[1]

With all else that it entails, shepherding primarily involves feeding and protecting the sheep. And both of these responsibilities are carried out in the same activities—the preaching and teaching of God's Word![2]

Through the course of church history, the nature of pastoral ministry evolved into a different animal. Around the beginning of the last century, the primary work of the pastor ultimately gravitated from the preaching event to the hands-on care of people and the administration of church programs. Today, pastors seem to be more interested in being CEOs, vision-casters, and large-group counselors. While all of these functions may have their proper place in pastoral work, the role of the pastor cries out for a biblical reformation. Specifically, it beckons us to return to the centrality of the preaching event, an event which is driven by a passion for the glory of God. We will call such a consideration a journey into *shepherdology*.

CHAPTER 4

The Shepherd's Stewardship:
GOOD STUFF OR GOD'S STUFF?

Many conservative men of God in our day have championed the cause of biblical inerrancy. However, some of those same well-meaning shepherds actually are *functional errantists!* They give the impression that they believe the Scriptures contain error, not by what they profess in their theology but by the way they handle the Bible in their preaching. Just because the Bible has God as its author, just because it carries His authority, and just because it wields His power to change lives, does not mean that He entrusted it to us for any and every use under the sun. If the shepherd overlooks this reality, his theology may be right while his preaching may be unbiblical.

If biblical shepherding is to be driven by a passion for God's glory, the awesomeness of the task demands that we give serious attention to the content of pastoral preaching. Like Paul, contemporary shepherds are bound to speak the testimony *of* God, not merely the testimony *about* God. Consequently, a right understanding of the testimony *of* God becomes all-important. We need to explore the philosophy of preaching stewardship in an effort to redeem the task from some unhealthy ideologies. Consider the following charges given to the shepherd who would venture to preach for God's glory.

Exalting God, Not Resourcing Man

For the past three decades, my own Southern Baptist denomination has been embroiled in a theological controversy surrounding our view of the Bible. While some shortsightedly have reacted to its political implications, the struggle largely has been a battle over the authority of the Scriptures. And it has been a battle that needed to be fought, for God's people in every generation must rise to guard and defend God's Word in the world. If we ever compromise the inerrancy and infallibility of the Bible, we weaken the very foundation on which the church is built.

As I have watched this controversy unfold, however, I have often wondered if there are not other equally crucial issues regarding the Scriptures that have been overlooked, especially when it comes to pastoral preaching. I am thinking specifically of the essence and agenda of the Bible. I am fearful that these issues will not get the attention they deserve. Hidden within these issues, however, is the understanding that the testimony *of God* was given primarily to exalt the Divine, not to resource mankind.

The Essence of the Bible

We live in a day in which people in churches are crying out for practical application and longing to see the relevance of the Bible. People have grown weary listening to sermons that only give them historical facts but provide them with no connection to real life.

Because we are a people of extremes, however, our humanity causes us to overreact to such abuses. And the result is that the pendulum swings to the opposite extreme of viewing the Bible merely as a resource manual for life on earth. And our infatuation with practical application has caused us to overlook the most important quality of the Bible—its *Divine feature*. We must understand that the Bible is God-centered, not man-centered. It is a book about Him more than it is a book about us. To make it otherwise is both selfish and arrogant. When we search God's Word with a how-to mentality, we often run right past the revelation of Almighty God. This perversion fits hand in glove with the order of contemporary culture: "It's all about me!"

The confusion regarding the essence of the Bible is compounded when applied to pastoral preaching, and the resulting deception is ever so subtle. Shepherds are ministers of grace and desire to meet people's needs and heal their hurts. But what happens when the Bible gives no specific and practical help for the life situations some of our people are facing? Among other things, the shepherd in his desire to help is tempted to find his preaching material from some place other than the Bible. Walter Kaiser lamented that many pastors have decided that using the Bible is a handicap for meeting the needs of the current generation and, therefore, "have gone to drawing their sermons from the plethora of recovery and pop-psychology books that fill our Christian bookstores."[1] Worse yet, the shepherd lowers himself to making the Bible say things it does not say. In an attempt to offer practical and helpful information, he stands up to say, "Thus saith the Lord," when the

Lord did not saith! How can God get the glory if the preacher does not speak what God says?

While the preaching described above cannot necessarily be categorized as heresy or even blatant error, neither can it be described as consisting of the inspired Word of God. In *Power in the Pulpit,* Jerry Vines and I described this subtlety as the often overlooked difference between *good stuff* and *God's stuff.*[2] The body of truth that is revealed in the Bible, given for the purpose of godliness (see 2 Pet. 1:2–4) and righteousness (see 2 Tim. 3:16), can be called *God's stuff.* It is the stuff of the Bible—its very essence. On the other hand, there is much helpful advice in life that is comprised of information or principles gleaned from simple observation and research. That is *good stuff.* Let us be very clear—the shepherd has not been charged with the task of speaking on all matters of *good stuff.*

While all truth is God's truth, not all truth has been included in His written Word. He has sovereignly chosen to include only that which is necessary for man's sanctification. There is a whole lot of good and helpful information in the world, but God did not choose to consecrate all of it as His inspired revelation necessary for spiritual transformation. In our previous work we cited the example of Aristotle, who delineated his principles of rhetoric simply by engaging in observation. He watched enough public speakers that he was able to glean certain "truths" for doing it effectively. The principles of rhetoric have had profound impact on preaching and all other forms of public speaking. But they are merely *good stuff.* Although they are both helpful and useful, they will not foster the God-life, much less glorify Him.

But the crisis we face in preaching today is not shepherds who deliver sermons on how to do good public speaking. The body of *good stuff* is far more appealing to contemporary churchgoers. That is what makes it so tough. If a therapist observes enough people dealing with stress on the job place, he will glean certain helpful principles for addressing the issue. If a marriage counselor observes enough people journeying through divorce recovery, she will be able to develop some guidelines that are helpful for that crisis. If parenting experts talk with enough moms and dads who are raising kids, they will be able to outline some practical ways for navigating such a task. And there will always be certain general truths in Scripture which can be applied to these and other life experiences.

The shepherd's authority to stand and speak "Thus saith the Lord" is not in *good stuff,* but *God's stuff.* While biblical truth surely informs certain principles that might be categorized as *good stuff,* its primary intent is more specific and far-reaching. The faithful shepherd will rightly interpret, exegete, and proclaim the truth of Scripture so as to allow it to accomplish its purpose in people's lives.

But when the shepherd prostitutes *God's stuff* for *good stuff,* anarchy occurs. And the biggest tragedy is not what people are *getting* but what they are *not getting.* While they certainly are getting some helpful information, they are being robbed of the truth that is necessary for realizing God's end and subsequently bringing glory to Him.

God's stuff is the very essence of the Bible. It is His book, and it is primarily about Him. When the preacher begins at this point in his interpretation and his application, then he is sure to exalt God and bring glory to His name. When he begins at the point of resourcing man regarding all of his questions and felt needs, however, his interpretation and application are certain to exalt humanity.

The Agenda of the Bible

In addition to the essence of the Bible, it is important for us to consider the agenda of the Bible. Scripture's agenda is more than merely resourcing mankind with pat answers and practical instructions. So it's not hard to find. In the study of Hebrew language, there exists a literary construction called an *inclusio.* An *inclusio* is where the same or similar beginning and end of a segment of literature hold the key to interpreting what is in the middle. While it would be a stretch to say that the Bible is an *inclusio* in the technical sense, the idea is helpful in uncovering God's agenda. The Scriptures do tell us of a very similar concept that characterizes the beginning and ending of the Word of God.

Consider the bookends of the Bible. The Bible opens with the declaration that "in the beginning God *created the heavens and the earth*" (Gen. 1:1, emphasis added). When the last pages of the Bible are turned, we behold the creation of "*a new heaven and a new earth,* for the first heaven and first earth had passed away" (Rev. 21:1, emphasis added). In essence creation and re-creation of heaven and earth serve to prop up the rest of Scripture.

This construction pleads with shepherds and all who read the Bible to look closely at its middle to determine God's agenda. Close consideration does not disappoint the diligent observer. At the risk of seeming like a Bible drill, let me take you on a journey that I believe reveals to us God's agenda in the Bible. This agenda, furthermore, will provide a framework within which shepherds and sheep can approach sermons freely and confidently for God's glory.

Our journey actually begins in eternity past. The apostle Paul told the Roman believers that the people whom God foreknew, "He also predestined *to be conformed to the image of His Son,* that He might be the firstborn among many brethren. Moreover whom He predestined, these He also called; whom He called, these He also justified; and whom He justified, these He also glorified" (Rom. 8:29–30; emphasis added). Before time began, God determined to save believers from their sins and set them on a course to be shaped into the image of His Son, Jesus Christ. Consequently, every believer is moving inescapably toward perfect righteousness as part of God's plan for Christ to reign throughout all eternity over a holy race made up of people who are citizens of His divine kingdom and children in His divine family.

When we step onto the pages of recorded history in the Bible, we are immediately introduced to the same theme. The creation of a physical dwelling place was only part of God's agenda. He determined to create for Himself an even more precious possession when He said, "Let Us make man in *Our* image, according to *Our* likeness; . . . So God created man in His *own* image; in the image of God He created him; male and female He created them" (Gen. 1:26–27, emphasis added). In the garden of Eden, God set in motion a plan to share Himself with His highest creation in eternal communion. The only way that was possible was for mankind to share in His likeness.

Something perverted God's agenda, however. Genesis 3 tells the paramount tragedy of the fall of God's precious creation. Sin entered the world and marred man's likeness to his Creator. The divine image, which provided the link to eternal communion with the Almighty, was distorted. The magnitude of the catastrophe is expressed in God's own words: "Behold, the man has become *like one of Us, to know good and evil.* And now, lest he put out his hand and take also of the tree of life, and eat, and live forever—" (Gen. 3:22, emphasis added). Only the Creator Himself can handle the knowledge of both good and evil. Only He can navigate such an understanding without succumbing to their abuse. As God's voice trails off of the pages of Scripture, the Bible reader is left with the distinct impression that God considered it absolutely unacceptable for mankind to remain in a state of corrupted likeness.

It is interesting to note the reference to the "tree of life" in this scenario. It is made without commentary or definition. The Bible first introduces it as the focal point of man's home, planted by God "in the midst of the garden" (Gen. 2:9). While we may never know the complete nature of the tree of life this side of heaven, we can surmise that partaking of its fruit apparently would have caused God's creatures to be cursed for eternity with the marred likeness to their Creator which characterized them at the time of consumption. This horrifying reality moved the gracious God to take action that would ensure the possibility of redemption. "So He drove out the man; and He placed cherubim at the east of the garden of Eden, and a flaming sword which turned every way, to guard the way to the tree of life" (Gen. 3:24).

What is incredibly fascinating, however, is that the tree of life noticeably disappears from the pages of God's Word after Genesis 3.[3] And guess where it shows up next? It reappears in the new heaven and the new earth at the very end of the Bible. In his vision of the New Jerusalem, the apostle John observed, "In the middle of its street, and on either side of the river, was the *tree of life,* which bore twelve fruits, each tree yielding its fruit every month. The leaves of the tree were for the healing of the nations" (Rev. 22:2, emphasis added). Amidst all of the mystery of the tree of life there exists an undeniable link between God's creation in Genesis and His re-creation in Revelation.

If the creation and re-creation of heaven and earth, with the tree of life in their midsts, serve as the bookends of the Bible, then the re-creation of mankind into the image of the Creator fills the pages in the middle. Even the Old Testament writers, with their limited understanding of the resurrection, looked for some restoration of God's likeness. The psalmist gladly acknowledged to God, "As for me, *I will see Your face* in righteousness; I shall be satisfied when I awake *in Your likeness*" (Ps. 17:15; emphasis added). His words no doubt were a precursor to those of the apostle John who said, "Beloved, now we are children of God; and it has not yet been revealed what we shall be, but we know that when He is revealed, we shall be *like Him,* for we shall *see Him* as He is" (1 John 3:2; emphasis added). After speaking of his vision of the tree of life in the New Jerusalem, John said of the saints, "They shall *see His face,* and His name shall be on their foreheads" (Rev. 22:4, emphasis added), an indication that they belong to Him (cf. Rev. 3:12; 7:3; 14:1).

The writings of the apostle Paul also are pregnant with this theme. He told the Corinthians that "we all, with unveiled face, beholding as in a mirror the glory of the Lord, are being transformed into *the same image from glory to glory*" (2 Cor. 3:18, emphasis added). He said to the Philippians that Christ Jesus "will transform our lowly body that it may be *conformed to His glorious body*" (Phil. 3:21, emphasis added). The Colossians were informed that they had "put on the new man who is renewed in knowledge according to *the image of Him who created him*" (Col. 3:10, emphasis added). Even Peter got in on the action, telling his readers that Jesus' "divine power has given to us all things that pertain to life and godliness, through the knowledge of Him who called us by glory and virtue, by which have been given to us exceedingly great and precious promises, that through these you may be *partakers of the divine nature*" (2 Pet. 1:3–4, emphasis added).

Did you notice that almost all of these references associate the re-created nature to the glory of God? Without question the inclusio of the Bible suggests to us that God is about the business of creating for Himself a dwelling place and a companion race for all eternity, both of which will reflect His glory. Revealing this mission is the obvious agenda of the Bible. Consequently, the task of both shepherd and sheep is to align themselves with that agenda and approach the preaching event accordingly. When God's agenda directs preaching in the church, then He is exalted and glorified.

Explaining Revelation, Not Revealing Information

Several years ago a well-known preacher in Oklahoma climbed up in a tower on a vigil after announcing that God had told him that if people did not send him eight million dollars, He was going to kill him! To most of us that seems absurd, but only because we measure the claim by the nature and oracles of God as revealed in the Bible. But what is the difference between that preacher's claim and the conservative evangelical shepherd who weights his sermons with declarations like "God told me" and "God is leading me" as authoritative underpinnings of extrabiblical information? Or what is the difference between his claim and the shepherd who draws the heart of his sermons from extrabiblical information as if to suggest that there are some things God did not think about regarding the needs of His people? At best we are putting words in God's mouth and insinuating to listeners that they are His! Such a horrific thought demands that we give some attention to where and how the shepherd gets his message, what he is supposed to do with it when he gets it, and why it is so important that he does it.

A Revelation about Revelation

"Why don't you get your messages from God?" I don't remember ever being as shocked in all of my ministry as I was when asked that question several weeks into my second pastorate. I had begun my ministry there preaching systematically through a book of the Bible. On that day, one of my Sunday School teachers came by my office and posed that question. He said there was no way I could be getting my messages from God because I just preached each week from the passage which followed the one from the week before.

What confused me most about his inquiry was the fact that I thought I *was* getting my messages from God! Because I also had begun preparation for doctoral work simultaneously with my new church ministry, I was rising about three o'clock in the morning every weekday in order to have time for prayer, study, and sermon preparation before fulfilling the expected office hours and other

duties of church administration. While there was always room for improvement, I really thought that I was going the extra mile to seek the Lord and be
spiritually prepared to feed His people. What I learned that day was that many
people who make up our congregations (as well as many of their shepherds!)
have a serious misunderstanding regarding the source of sermon content.

My Sunday School teacher went on to tell me that many of his previous
pastors did not ever get their messages until they were on the way from their
office to the pulpit on Sunday mornings! This "preacher as pope" mentality
assumes that God has extrabiblical revelation for His people on a weekly basis
and that He communicates it to the shepherd through some mystical means
that is often articulated as "getting a Word" from Him. In fact, many preachers
and parishioners see this occurrence of omnipotent osmosis as displacing the
need for Bible study and sermon preparation.

This notion is furthered by the looseness with which many preachers throw
around those phrases like "God told me" and "The Lord said to me." This scenario is frighteningly similar to God's analysis of the prophets of Jeremiah's day:

> I have heard what the prophets have said who prophesy lies in
> My name, saying, "I have dreamed, I have dreamed!" How long
> will this be in the heart of the prophets who prophesy lies?
> Indeed they are prophets of the deceit of their own heart, who
> try to make My people forget My name by their dreams which
> everyone tells his neighbor, as their fathers forgot My name for
> Baal.
>
> "The prophet who has a dream, let him tell a dream;
> And he who has My word, let him speak My word faithfully.
> What is the chaff to the wheat?" says the LORD.
> "Is not My word like a fire?" says the LORD,
> "And like a hammer that breaks the rock in pieces?"
>
> "Therefore behold, I am against the prophets," says the LORD,
> "who steal My words every one from his neighbor. Behold, I am
> against the prophets," says the LORD, "who use their tongues
> and say, 'He says.' Behold, I am against those who prophesy
> false dreams," says the LORD, "and tell them, and cause My
> people to err by their lies and by their recklessness. Yet I did
> not send them or command them; therefore they shall not profit
> this people at all," says the LORD (Jer. 23:25–32).

In addition to deceptively turning people's attention from the legitimate Words of God, such preaching frustrates individuals who do not hear God as "audibly." These false shepherds imply that God has a steady diet of extrabiblical revelation that is necessary for His people's well-being, and that only they as the "Lord's anointed" can provide it. And this erroneous preaching results in reckless living that leads to no profit.

The nature of shepherding today involves the issue of credibility. If preacher's today can say "Thus saith the Lord," and by it place extrabiblical information on the same plane as scriptural truth, then our listeners have no standard by which to determine the validity of truth. If pastors today are still responsible for "getting a word from God" that no one has ever heard, then we have no basis by which to distinguish the one heralding heresy from the one transmitting truth. The example of the Bereans should be noted because they searched their Scriptures to see whether or not Paul's words could be substantiated by them (see Acts 17:11).

If we believe revelation is progressive and that God is still in the process of revealing information necessary for His people's spiritual well-being, then the Bible is no more than one among many sources from which the preacher draws an authoritative word from on high. But if the shepherd sees the Bible as God's total and final revelation of truth that is necessary for accomplishing His agenda, then his responsibility is simply to report it to the people. He is relieved from the mythical notion that he is responsible for revealing God's truth to people. Furthermore, he can spend his time learning to be a better reporter of biblical truth rather than a suave revelator of new information.

An Explanation about Explanation

The idea of a contemporary shepherd revealing new information obviously is the reflection of a very common yet grossly nonbiblical theology of revelation and inspiration. This error easily perverts people's understanding of the shepherd's responsibility as a preacher, especially if they do not process how preaching has evolved from being *revelatory* in the biblical period to being *explanatory* today.

We must understand that the role of the preacher in the postapostolic age is of a fundamentally different nature than that of preachers in every preceding generation. This may be one of the most overlooked factors in determining models for contemporary homiletics and hermeneutics, for that matter. During the biblical period preachers like Jesus—as well as the Old and New Testament prophets and the apostles—often practiced what we might call *revelatory* preaching. They proclaimed God's first-time revelation as they spoke. In other words, they spoke information from God that man had never heard before. It was new stuff! Additionally, these preachers also did some *explanatory* preaching during their ministries. After new stuff from God had been given, they frequently provided explanation of the previously revealed information as people returned to it time and time again.[4] Both their revelatory and explanatory preaching were characterized by Spirit-directed persuasion as they appealed to people to respond to God's words in the affirmative.

At the close of the biblical period, however, preaching naturally evolved to the point of being only explanatory in nature. The "apostles' doctrine" was canonized along with the Old Testament Scriptures to form our Bible. While continuing to be characterized by passionate persuasion, all postapostolic proclamation possessed this explanatory nature as the essence of its very being. The closing of the Canon evidenced the end of God's revelation of "new stuff" regarding that which is necessary for true life and godliness (see 2 Pet. 1:4–5). Consequently, every preacher from that point forward ceased to have the responsibility of introducing—or *revealing*—new information from God. Postapostolic preachers should merely explain that which God has already revealed and persuade people to act on it.

Explanation of the biblical text is so vital because the Bible is the source of the knowledge of God's truth (see 2 Tim. 3:14–17; 1 Pet. 2:2). The Word of God is both the road map that leads people to salvation and the food that fuels their re-creation into Christ's image. How fast believers grow depends totally on how much truth they embrace and apply to their lives. The only way they can get that truth is to understand it, either by studying it personally or by having someone explain it to them. Consequently, the ultimate end of preaching should be to conform the believer to the image of the One who created him.

There will never be any growth in the Christian life apart from knowledge (see Rom. 12:2; Eph. 4:22). Holy living flows from mature knowledge, and mature knowledge comes only by explanation. This suggests that the contemporary shepherd's responsibility is not to "wow" his flock each week with something new that no one has ever heard before. Instead, he is to wrestle with the text of Scripture until he determines God's intended meaning, help his people grasp it by way of clear and intentional explanation, and persuade them to act upon it through passionate persuasion.

Today people seem to be much more interested in personal experience, emotional feeling, and pragmatic application than explanation of the biblical text. The de-emphasis on explanation in preaching highlights the willingness of listeners to accept uninformed application which they readily put to use in their lives. Many shepherds are more than ready to accommodate. As long as listeners identify with the message experientially, walk away with a better feeling about themselves and their lives, or glean some principle or instruction for dealing with their current circumstance, then no one is really concerned about whether or not it makes sense or is based upon truth. The only thing that will turn the tide will be for shepherds to be faithful stewards of God's call to be explainers of His Word and for those who listen to them to demand help in gaining such understanding.

Shepherds are no longer responsible for *revelatory* preaching but solely responsible for persuasive *explanatory* preaching. The default approach to preaching is simply to explain and apply what God has already revealed in His Word.

An Understanding about Understanding

Explanation in contemporary preaching is not an end in and of itself, however. Explanation is a means to an end, and the end of the matter is understanding. The reason explanation is vitally important in preaching is because people must be helped to understand the truth of God's Word. Modern listeners do not need a new word from God. They need to understand the Word He has already given them! God's commentary on His children in Hosea's day was a direct rebuke of the shepherds who failed to help them know and understand His Word: "My people are destroyed for lack of knowledge. Because you have rejected knowledge, I also will reject you from being priest for Me; because you have forgotten the law of your God, I also will forget your children" (Hos. 4:6). People's understanding of the Bible is critical in their relationship with God.

The relationship between understanding truth and a person's re-creation into Christlikeness is also crucial. Bill Hull observed that "transformation comes through the commitment of the mind. Without the proper knowledge and thinking we have no basis for personal change or growth. The mind is the pivotal starting place for change."[5] And the great doctrines of the Bible imply that man has an inescapable obligation both to think and act on what he knows.

Both the Old and New Testaments underscore the necessity of understanding God's Word. During the great revival of Israel's worship recorded in Nehemiah 8, Ezra and the other teachers placed great emphasis on the people's understanding of the Scriptures. The text indicates that everyone "who could hear with understanding" and "who could understand" (Neh. 8:2–3) was gathered for the event. Men, women, and apparently some children were included in the service based upon their ability to understand what was to be spoken. Understanding was so important that the ability to comprehend the truth was at least one criteria for participation!

Further in the passage Nehemiah pointed out what the teachers did in order to explain the Scriptures so the people could understand with their minds. First, "they read distinctly from the book" (Neh. 8:8). They did not just "bottom line" the Scriptures. They knew it was important for people to make the connection between what the teachers said about each passage and what the people knew to be the authoritative document. Even in a biblically illiterate, postmodern culture, there still is enough credence given to the Bible, even if just token, that it merits showing people where you get your contentions. Making this connection is a key to explanation and right understanding.

Second, these teachers in Nehemiah "gave the sense" (Neh. 8:8), which is likely a reference to translating the Scriptures from Hebrew to Aramaic. In captivity, the Jews would have used Aramaic because it was the international diplomatic language of the day much like English is in our day. Consequently, part of the work of the Levites would have been to give the people an Aramaic translation. But "translation" always involves more than just moving from one language to another. All translations involve interpretation to some degree. And that is what these teachers did—they interpreted the Scripture for the people so they could understand it. The root word here means "to break up" paragraph by paragraph. Essentially, these guys were revealing God's intended meaning of the Scripture that had been covered up by language, time, culture, social setting, and other factors so that they "helped them to understand" (Neh. 8:8).

The New Testament follows suit with the same emphasis. The two disciples on the road to Emmaus were "foolish ones, and slow of heart to believe in all that the prophets have spoken!" (Luke 24:25). But then Jesus explained the Scriptures and helped them to understand them: "And beginning at Moses and all the Prophets, He expounded to them in all the Scriptures the things concerning Himself" (Luke 24:27). And right understanding of God's Word makes supernatural impact, for "they said to one another, 'Did not our heart burn within us while He talked with us on the road, and while He opened the Scriptures to us?'" (Luke 24:32). God's Word, rightly understood, does something to the human heart!

The apostle Paul indicated that the Holy Spirit brings about life transformation by "the renewing of your mind" (Rom. 12:2). And he kept hammering the same thing home in his ministry to the Colossians, "warning every man and teaching every man in all wisdom, that we may present every man perfect in

Christ Jesus" (Col. 1:28). By receiving Christ as Lord and Savior, he told them, we "have put on the new man who is renewed in knowledge according to the image of Him who created him" (Col. 3:10). Consequently, he charged them to "let the word of Christ dwell in you richly in all wisdom, teaching and admonishing one another" (Col. 3:16).

Such is the responsibility of the contemporary Christian shepherd. His primary task is not to give opinions, indirect implications, or extrabiblical principles but instead to reveal the Holy Spirit's intended meaning in Scripture so that people's minds are exposed to supernatural truth and their lives are transformed into the image of Jesus Christ. Right explanation and understanding are the beginning point of life transformation.

Edifying Churches, Not Reaching Seekers

For all practical purposes the modern church growth movement was launched in 1955 with the publication of Donald McGavran's *Bridges of God.* By the end of the 1970s, a flood of other books, along with a host of seminars, conferences, programs, and organizations, were available to shepherds and church leaders. To say the least, the subject has monopolized the church's attention since that time. Still today we seem to be consumed with learning, teaching, and discussing principles and methods that will produce church growth. While many of these efforts are to be commended, it is horrifying at times to observe the disconnect between some of them and the clear biblical teaching on the subject. One of the most disturbing trends in the contemporary church is displacing edification of the body with unchecked efforts to reach so-called seekers. It is not at all a stretch to say that this has become the order of the day.

Now before I venture any further into the present discussion, let me make something very clear. I am all about evangelism. I do not believe there is anything more important for individual believers or the church body to be doing during our time in this world than to be aggressively and passionately proclaiming Jesus as both God and Savior that men, women, boys, and girls might miss hell and make heaven. Doing evangelism and missions is just about the only thing in which the church engages now that it will not be able to do a whole lot better when we get to heaven. That says to me that it ought to be a top priority for us right now. But the increasing popularity of seeker-driven methodologies and contradicting biblical teaching on the subject obligates shepherds and their people to ask two questions: *What is Jesus' strategy for church growth?* and *What is the role of the shepherd in that strategy?*

The Savior on Church Growth

When I was being interviewed by the leadership of the congregation I now have the privilege of shepherding, I was asked a similar question on a couple of different occasions—*What will you do to grow this church?* My answer was always the same. I told them that I could and would do nothing to grow the church. Such is a task that is beyond my human ability—and my biblical responsibility!

When Jesus, likely pointing to Himself, announced to Peter that "on this rock I will build My church," He declared the most fundamental truth about church growth—it is His deal! Jesus made it very clear that He alone builds the church. Regardless of our good intentions, any claim that we make or effort that we put forth regarding growing a church is competing with the Lord.

Our modern obsession with church growth tells us differently. We outline strategies, hold seminars, develop training programs, all designed to enhance our supposed effectiveness in growing churches. And certainly it is possible to win converts to an organization, a movement, a cause, and especially to a personality. All it takes is some good business principles, personal charisma, human reason, or skillful persuasion. But no one other than Jesus will ever be able to win someone to His church. Jesus said, "All that the Father gives Me will come to Me" (John 6:37).

During my first pastorate I learned a lesson that has haunted me my entire ministry. I recall being with some of my fellow pastors on occasions when none of our church members were around, like weekly ministers' conferences and summer camps. As a young man in ministry, I remember being shocked to hear some of them use language or tell jokes that they would never think of letting their church members hear roll off of their lips. And some of these guys were pastoring large, growing churches. The thing that has stayed with me is the realization that, by all the standards we use to measure church growth, it is possible to be "successful" in ministry and all the time be doing it in the flesh! But authentic church growth is the sovereign work of Jesus Christ. Human effort can produce human results, but only Christ can produce divine results.

The early church is a testimony to the work of Christ in church growth. During his Pentecost sermon, Peter declared that Christ builds His church from "as many as the Lord our God will call" (Acts 2:39). While evangelism and church growth are mentioned in the narrative of the infant church, they do not show up until the very last sentence of the chapter when Luke notes that "the Lord added to the church daily those who were being saved" (Acts 2:47). The language of the New Testament here indicates that this growth was something enacted upon the church from an outside force, namely the Lord (see also Acts 5:14; 11:24).

As the gospel spread outside of Jerusalem, the same understanding was prevalent. When Paul and Barnabas preached at Pisidian Antioch, "as many as had been appointed to eternal life believed" (Acts 13:48). Jesus encouraged Paul when he was under pressure at Corinth by saying, "Do not be afraid, but speak, and do not keep silent; for I am with you, and no one will attack you to hurt you; for I have many people in this city" (Acts 18:9–10). The true and faithful preaching of the apostles was not even capable by itself of saving people and bringing them into the church. Only those whose hearts had been sovereignly massaged by the truth of God's Word were added to the church.

Church growth is *His* doing. And any principle, program, strategy, or methodology that displaces His approach in any way actually is working against the efforts of Christ to build His church. If we want to see God build churches against which the gates of Hades will not prevail, we better be content with letting Him build them the way He has determined to do so.

The Shepherd in Church Growth

Healthy people make up healthy congregations, and Jesus seems to deposit the people He is saving into healthy congregations. The apostle Paul expounded on the specifics of Jesus' plan for church growth and showed how nurturing the body's health contributed to its growth. He told them that Jesus

> Himself gave some *to be* apostles, some prophets, some evan-
> gelists, and some pastors and teachers, for the equipping of the
> saints for the work of ministry, for the edifying of the body of
> Christ, till we all come to the unity of the faith and of the
> knowledge of the Son of God, to a perfect man, to the measure
> of the stature of the fullness of Christ; that we should no longer
> be children, tossed to and fro and carried about with every wind
> of doctrine, by the trickery of men, in the cunning craftiness of
> deceitful plotting, but, speaking the truth in love, may grow up
> in all things into Him who is the head—Christ—from whom the
> whole body, joined and knit together by what every joint sup-
> plies, according to the effective working by which every part
> does its share, causes growth of the body for the edifying of
> itself in love (Eph. 4:11–16).

While acknowledging Jesus as the divine church grower, Paul expounds on the Master's plan by identifying its ultimate goal and the human instruments used to accomplish it. It involves the edification—*building up*—of His body into His image through the ministry of His Word. That is what a shepherd can contribute to church growth—nourishing people to spiritual health by feeding them God's Word. The shepherd can't grow the church, but he can foster growth in the people by feeding them supernatural truth!

Paul introduces the gifted men whom Jesus gave to the church as catalysts for setting His plan in motion (see Eph. 4:11). The spiritual gifts given by Jesus to His church include both those gifts given to individual believers and those gifted men given to the church. The apostles and prophets, who were given strictly for New Testament times, were followed respectively by the gifted men called evangelists and pastor-teachers. These two offices are given for continuing ministry to the church. It is the plan of Jesus for evangelists and pastor-teachers to equip, build up, and develop His church as outlined in the rest of the passage. Along with evangelists, then, teaching shepherds are the agents that Christ uses to initiate the church growth process.

Jesus' plan for church growth is very simple: "equipping" leads to "the work of the ministry" which leads to "the edifying of the body of Christ" (Eph. 4:12). The ignition point of this plan comes at the hands of evangelists and teaching shepherds in the equipping of God's people for service. As God's people are equipped for service, the by-product is the natural growth of the body into "the measure of the stature of the fullness of Christ" (Eph. 4:13). This is the capsulization of Jesus' plan for church growth.

The language used to describe the specific activity which is assigned to these two office gifts further supports God's intention. In the language of the New Testament, the word translated *equipping* basically refers to that which is fit, restored to its original condition, or made complete. The word frequently was used as a medical term for the setting of bones and thus something that was put back like it was supposed to be. New Testament writers used it to describe both the spiritual maturity of the individual believer (e.g., 2 Cor. 13:11; Heb. 13:20–21) and the corporate unification of the body (e.g., 1 Cor. 1:10).

All of this talk of restoration into an original condition should strike a familiar cord with us. Do you remember our earlier discussion about the agenda of the Bible and God's work of restoring His creation? Here Paul turned us on to how that plays out when the body gathers together. Evangelists and teaching shepherds are endowed with certain spiritual gifts that enable them to equip God's children for service. As they are equipped, each individual believer makes a contribution which "causes growth of the body for the edifying of itself in love" (Eph. 4:16).

The roles of these two office gifts are similar yet distinct. The evangelist, whose work has mistakenly been limited over the years to itinerant ministry, has a twofold purpose. First and foremost, he is specially gifted to help people understand the gospel and lead them to receive Jesus as God and Savior. Second, the context of the passage indicates that he also is responsible for equipping God's people to do the same. Shepherds, or pastor-teachers, subsequently have the same responsibilities, yet with somewhat of a reversal of emphases. First and foremost, they are specially gifted to provide the leadership and spiritual resources that cause those who are being saved to be conformed into the image of Christ. Second, they are called upon to do the work of the evangelist (see 2 Tim. 4:5). Together, these two offices serve as the primary equipping platforms for authentic church growth.

The Stewardship of Church Growth

Jesus' model also makes so much more sense when it comes to the stewardship of the church's energy and resources. We hear much today about targeting the most number of lost people. Many churches are relocating to rapidly growing areas where there are large pockets of the population. Other churches speak of tailoring worship services to make them more palatable to seekers. Certainly the evangelistic motive behind such efforts is commendable. But the question must be asked, *Where will the most number of lost people always be, inside or outside the church?* The answer is obvious. As strategically located as our churches may be, as seeker-friendly as we may make them, reality is that most lost people will never darken the doors of our church buildings.

Consequently, the church is much better served in applying most of its evangelistic energy and resources to preparing believers to penetrate the marketplace with the gospel. The most number of lost people will be confronted with the gospel as God's people are educated and equipped for proclaiming Jesus as Savior and God in the marketplace. Such is the Great Commission, "As you go, make disciples" (cf. Matt. 28:19, author's paraphrase). This should include motivation and training for both personal witness and public proclamation. And our changing culture is going to require us to think strategically about how to gain a hearing in the various venues of the church scattered, not simply coloring outside the lines but thinking of new colors. When the church comes together, however, it is wise to apply most of its energy and resources to the authentic worship of the living God by His people, including their edification through the teaching of the Bible.

Once again, we find ourselves back to the magnitude of the shepherd's stewardship—the proclamation of *God's stuff* as opposed to mere *good stuff.* Our most earnest effort should be given to preaching the Bible by "warning every man and teaching every man in all wisdom, that we may present every man *perfect* in Christ Jesus" (Col. 1:28; emphasis added). So "preach the word," beloved shepherd! "Be ready in season and out of season. Convince, rebuke, exhort, with all longsuffering and teaching" (2 Tim. 4:2). And dear church member, replace your itching ears with a hunger and thirst for righteousness. Together, then, shepherd and people will be sure to edify and build up the body into the image of Christ according to His plan for church growth.

Where Do I Go from Here . . .

Now that you have ventured into the philosophy of shepherding, you may proceed one of two ways as indicated by the shaded areas on the chart below. The (▼) symbol indicates the thematic development of more of these philosophical considerations. If you are following this path, proceed to chapter 5, "The Shepherd's Power." The (➡) symbol indicates the continued development of the *content* of preaching from these beginning philosophical considerations on to their practical implications. If you are following this path, proceed to chapter 7, "Preaching as Worship." Before beginning chapter 7, however, be sure to read the introduction to part 3, "Passion-Driven Sermonology."

Table 4.1

	PART 1 (Biblical)		PART 2 (Philosophical)		PART 3 (Practical)
(Content)	Chapter 1: The Message of Preaching ▼	➡	Chapter 4: The Shepherd's Stewardship ▼	➡	Chapter 7: Preaching as Worship ▼
(Resource)	Chapter 2: The Means for Preaching ▼	➡	Chapter 5: The Shepherd's Power ▼	➡	Chapter 8: Preaching with Potency ▼
(Goal)	Chapter 3: The Motive in Preaching	➡	Chapter 6: The Shepherd's Relevance	➡	Chapter 9: Preaching for Eternity

CHAPTER 5

The Shepherd's Power:
SUBJECTIVE OR OBJECTIVE?

You may have been watching several years ago on New Year's Day when a beautiful float in the Tournament of Roses parade suddenly sputtered and quit. It was out of gas. The whole parade was held up until someone could get a can of gas. The amusing and ironic thing about the whole deal was this float represented the Standard Oil Company. With its vast oil resources, the float belonging to the company who makes gas was out of gas! Some people are saying the same thing about modern preaching. Few would argue with the fact that the preaching event represents the Christian church. But backed by its vast spiritual resources, the medium of communication that uniquely belongs to the church—the possessor of all spiritual power (see Eph. 1:15–23)—often seems like it is bankrupt of potency! When the parade of evangelicalism passes before the world, the pulpit oftentimes sputters and quits. Where has the power gone?

The teaching shepherd has an advantage that separates him from all other public communicators. While even secular public speakers can be passionate about their subject matter, one particular ingredient is reserved solely for the one who speaks the Words of God. This ingredient has been called the *anointing*. Without a doubt anointed preaching places God into the sermon and on the preacher. When a shepherd preaches in the power of God, the results are remarkable and sometimes even unexplainable. But while most shepherds would agree that anointing is indispensable in preaching, many have struggled to determine its secret. Hence, the question of the ages for most of us who preach, *From whence comes the anointing?*

While many have suggested that the answer to that question is the subjective aspect of the preaching event, I would propose that it may be more objective than we think. Consider this. We know that the Holy Spirit has bound Himself to the Holy Scriptures. Consequently, as a holy shepherd binds himself to the Holy Scriptures, he by default will be binding himself to the Holy Spirit and His power. In other words, the shepherd, the Spirit, and the Scripture work in holy concert with one another to host the anointing of God in preaching. Thus, the anointing is within the grasp of every Christian shepherd and provides the means by which he engages in powerful preaching! Here's what makes it work.

The Work of the Shepherd

We live in a day in which great emphasis is being placed on human ability, wisdom, and methodology in the Christian communication field. We argue over which rhetorical form speaks to postmodern listeners. Preachers are desperate to plug into the communication approaches of the entertainment world and other "successful" secular venues. They take desperate measures to analyze audiences and then align their own presentations to their preferences. Although some consideration should be given to all of these areas, the emphasis that is placed on them frequently leads to a disconnect between an understanding of the demonstration of God's power and the shepherd's role in the preaching event. All too often the shepherd is tempted to actually depend upon himself or other human means to impact the lives of listeners.

Consequently, I would like to submit that the shepherd does play a very unique, yet interdependent, role in demonstrating the power of God in the preaching event. In the previous chapter we noted how the role of preaching had evolved from being revelatory, explanatory, and persuasive during the days of the prophets, Jesus, and the apostles to simply being explanatory and persuasive today. Obviously, the common denominators in that evolution are explanation and persuasion. Having already addressed the role of the shepherd as *explainer* of God's Word, we need to talk about his role as *persuader* as it relates to preaching influence and power.

The Influence of Persuasion

Without a doubt Bible preachers were persuaders. Although the apostle Paul said he refused to utilize "persuasive words of *human* wisdom" (1 Cor. 2:4, emphasis added), he never said he refused to use *persuasion*! In fact, a holistic analysis of his journeys and his writings reveals that he obviously did not object to the use of "persuasive words" themselves (see Acts 13:43; 17:4–5; 18:4; 19:26; 28:24; 2 Cor. 5:11). He knew that persuasion was one of the most important elements in preaching. The primary New Testament verb means "to use words to persuade others to believe." Paul and Barnabas spoke to Christian converts and *"persuaded* them to continue in the grace of God" (Acts 13:43, emphasis added). Upon his arrival in Corinth, Paul "reasoned in the synagogue every Sabbath, and *persuaded* both Jews and Greeks" (Acts 18:4, emphasis added). Later he would claim to the Corinthians, "Knowing, therefore, the terror of the Lord, we *persuade* men" (2 Cor. 5:11, emphasis added). The particular word used in that statement means "to persuade or to induce one with words to believe."

There is no argument that persuasive speech techniques have had tremendous influence on Christian preaching. Classical rhetoric probably has shaped the way we preach more than any other single secular influence. Aristotle systematized an approach to persuasive speaking in his *On Rhetoric,* written around the middle of the fourth century B.C. His material has been a seminal work in the field of rhetoric since that time. He defined *rhetoric* "as the faculty of discovering all the possible means of persuasion in any subject."[1] Along with Cicero and Quintillan, he systematically developed rhetorical theory.

At first, ancient oratory and rhetoric impacted Christian preaching chiefly at the point of form and mechanics. Greco-Roman oratory had a moral tone but lacked religious content. Christian preaching contained the religious content and added the didactic element in its presentation. As Christians were taught to communicate the gospel, they naturally applied the respective rules. This natural relationship between rhetoric and preaching continued to mature through the years. Leaders in the Christian church were trained in Greek tradition, and the canons of rhetoric were applied to all aspects of the preaching event. Augustine, who was a teacher of rhetoric, produced the first notable work on homiletics with *On Christian Doctrine.* The work applied rhetorical principles to Christian proclamation.

After Augustine, the emphasis on persuasion in homiletics waned for approximately fifteen hundred years. But toward the end of the nineteenth century, several notable homileticians began incorporating rhetorical principles into their writings. John A. Broadus's work *A Treatise on the Preparation and Delivery of Sermons* in 1870 became the authoritative work on homiletics in the United States. His outline and content were influenced heavily by rhetorical principles. Other homileticians followed Broadus's lead. Austin Phelps believed homiletics to be a species of rhetoric. His book, *The Theory of Preaching,* was developed almost entirely on rhetorical theory.

Throughout the course of church history, numerous evangelical preachers have been unashamedly instructed how to prepare and deliver sermons in the rhetorical tradition. My own denomination is a classic example. About our paradigm of homiletical instruction, Chuck Kelley observed:

> Invention, arrangement, style, delivery, and memory became
> the organizational framework for teaching students how to
> preach. From the beginning, Southern Baptists were taught to
> link biblical proclamation with rhetorical intent. Proclaim the
> Word of God with a view to persuading men and women to
> respond to God's call for repentance, faith, and obedience.[2]

Without question, the form of the sermon and the call for response have been just a few of the logical results of the rhetorical emphasis on homiletical theory and practice.

The Independence of Preaching

The influence of persuasive speech on preaching, however, doesn't mean the *nature* of pulpit persuasion is the same as that in secular venues. While Paul may have been a master persuader, he realized that Christian persuasion was independent of the Greco-Roman rhetoric of his day because it was dependent upon something entirely different for its force. And contemporary shepherds who desire to preach persuasively, as well as those who listen to them, must understand that independence in light of the numerous manipulative and coercive communication methods so common in our day. While we can be sure that Paul was influenced by the art of persuasion that permeated Hellenistic life, he obviously employed a dimension of persuasion that transformed and even subverted his rhetorical tradition.[3]

The shepherd's influence and power in the preaching event must be distinguished from the persuasion of secular orators in two interdependent ways. I will mention them briefly at this point and then develop each one respectively in the remaining two sections of the chapter. First, while secular orators depend upon their own persuasive and argumentative resources, the Christian preacher never speaks on his own authority. He solely rests in the authority of someone else. Thompson observed:

> Like the public reader of Paul's letters, the Christian preacher
> acts in Paul's absence, interpreting his words for the believing
> community. The authority does not belong to the preacher, but
> to Paul. . . . Christian preaching involves an authoritative word
> from God that is mediated by the preacher.[4]

This reality has enormous implications for the content of contemporary preaching. Any influencing power that the modern shepherd may have is determined by the supernatural Word of God.

For us today, it is not only the words of Paul but also those of Moses, David, Isaiah, Matthew, Mark, Luke, John, and all of the other biblical writers. We speak only on their authority as they spoke only on the authority of the Holy Spirit of God. Peter said:

> And so we have the prophetic word confirmed, which you do
> well to heed as a light that shines in a dark place, until the day
> dawns and the morning star rises in your hearts; knowing this
> first, that no prophecy of Scripture is of any private interpreta-
> tion, for prophecy never came by the will of man, but holy
> men of God spoke as they were moved by the Holy Spirit
> (2 Pet. 1:19–21).

Contemporary preachers, then, deny any dependence on the resources of secular orators but totally rely on the authority of the Bible. Anything else would result only in glory for the preacher.

The preacher's persuasion is distinguished from secular orators in a second way. The Christian shepherd has a relationship with his audience that assumes the Holy Spirit's conviction is at work in the listeners. Paul's relationship to his listeners was radically different from that of his secular counterparts. While he often used standard forms of Aristotelian argumentation, his primary basis of authority was his role as apostle (e.g., 1 Cor. 1:1; 2:6–16) and father to his young children in the faith (e.g., 1 Thess. 2:11–12).[5] Such an approach flies in the face of Greco-Roman rhetoric! George Kennedy noted that both Matthew and Paul "make extensive use of the forms of logical argument, but the validity of their arguments is entirely dependent on their assumptions, which cannot be logically and objectively proved."[6] In other words, they could only be understood by those who were aided by the Spirit of God!

In a very real sense, then, contemporary preaching is the authoritative preaching of the prophetic tradition, resting on the Word of God and the work of the Holy Spirit. We do not fight with ordinary human weapons of rational persuasion but with weapons that are divinely powerful for pulling down strongholds in our efforts to take every thought captive to Christ (cf. 2 Cor. 10:4). Christian preaching is ultimately rooted in the apostolic authority that is mediated by the apostolic witness of the New Testament Scriptures, a witness that affirmed and confirmed the same authority for the Old Testament Canon.

Today shepherds mediate authoritative instruction to the church through the Spirit-anointed teaching and preaching of the supernatural Word of God. As heirs of the prophetic tradition, they simply recall the words of those who spoke the very words of God. The teaching shepherd does not speak for himself, but he speaks as a "steward" whose task it is to be faithful in upholding what has been given to him.[7] The degree of his persuasive influence is in direct proportion to the authority of the Word that he proclaims and the activity of the Holy Spirit in that proclamation. So let's develop these two distinctives so we can preach and listen to preaching with a dependence upon God's influence. Then He'll get the glory for it!

The Work of the Scriptures

God's shepherds must understand that the very stewardship entrusted to them is also their only hope of demonstrating His Spirit and power in order to effect lasting life change in listeners. Charles Spurgeon said:

> The power that is in the Gospel does not lie in the eloquence of
> the preacher, otherwise men would be the converters of souls,
> nor does it lie in the preacher's learning, otherwise it would
> consist in the wisdom of men. We might preach until our
> tongues rotted, till we would exhaust our lungs and die, but
> never a soul would be converted unless the Holy Spirit be with
> the Word of God to give it the power to convert the soul.[8]

Our God-breathed Christian Scriptures are the very source of life-changing power in preaching. And as the shepherd is faithful to proclaim them, God's Spirit will demonstrate His power in transforming people and permeating their lives! Consider the role of Scripture in the matter.

Completing the Pastor

The most pregnant and succinct passage in all of the Bible regarding the work of Scripture in preaching for life change has to be 2 Timothy 3:14–17. Above all others, this text demands our careful consideration. In it the apostle Paul appealed to Timothy's spiritual heritage and pleaded with the young shepherd to

> continue in the things which you have learned and been assured
> of, knowing from whom you have learned them, and that from
> childhood you have known the Holy Scriptures, which are able
> to make you *wise for salvation* through faith which is in Christ

Jesus. All Scripture is given by inspiration of God, and is
profitable for *doctrine,* for *reproof,* for *correction,* for *instruction in righteousness,* that the man of God may be *complete,*
thoroughly equipped for every good work (2 Tim. 3:14–17,
emphasis added).

Here Paul renders the inspired Scripture capable of providing everything that
is needed for life and godliness (cf. 2 Pet. 1:2–4).

The Bible is clear that this is the Spirit's work. The phrase "inspiration of
God" (2 Tim. 3:16) is a compound adjective ("God" and "breathe") used only
here in the New Testament—all Scripture is God-breathed! The apostle Peter
specifically defined this breath of God as the Holy Spirit when he said that
Scripture "never came by the will of man, but holy men of God spoke as they
were moved by the Holy Spirit" (2 Pet. 1:21). Jesus was well aware that the men
He commissioned to write the Gospels would not be able to recall accurately
everything He said and did. So He promised that "the Helper, the Holy Spirit,
whom the Father will send in My name, He will teach you all things, and bring
to your remembrance all things that I said to you" (John 14:26; see also
15:26–27). Essentially the breath of God is the Spirit of God.

But let's not allow our familiarity with the text to cause us to overlook an
important reality for shepherds. Are Paul's words here merely delineating the
supernatural effectualness of Scripture for *all* people? Look again. The apostle
is talking specifically about "the man of God" (2 Tim. 3:17)! This is a technical
phrase used only of Timothy in the New Testament but frequently in the Old
Testament for those who proclaimed the Word of God. As we will shortly see,
the Scriptures certainly possess great blessing and benefit for all who will hear
and heed them. But Paul is speaking specifically in this text of Scripture's special value for shepherds who proclaim God's Word.

So how does the Bible equip the shepherd to preach the Bible? First, it
makes him "complete" (2 Tim. 3:17). This means he will have everything he
needs to be able to fulfill his calling, specifically the aspect of preaching
(cf. Col. 2:10). The Word of God essentially is all the man of God needs to be
able to carry out his ministry effectively. Second, it makes him "equipped for
every good work," to meet all the demands that being a faithful steward of
God's Word may bring his way. The shepherd who carefully studies, sincerely
believes, diligently obeys, and faithfully teaches the truths of Scripture will
stand strong in proclaiming, living, and defending the faith. Most of all, the
"equipped" shepherd will be able to equip the saints for the work of the ministry so the body can grow up into Christ (see Eph. 4:11–16).

In the verses preceding 2 Timothy 2:17, Paul identifies five particular benefits of the "Holy Scriptures" that, in the hands of the faithful steward, enable him to shepherd his people with supernatural, life-changing power. First, *Scripture provides wisdom for all godliness.* Paul asserts that the Old Testament is "able to make you wise for salvation through faith which is in Christ Jesus" (2 Tim. 3:15). First and foremost, his reference here identifies Scripture's ability to point the way to justification. But Paul also was including here the aspects of sanctification and glorification. Young Timothy already was a believer and, therefore, justified. In the language of the New Testament, Paul uses a verb tense that suggests the wisdom given by Scripture was a reality through the whole process of salvation. Dear shepherd, the inspired Word of God in your hands and mouth contains the wisdom people need in order to come to know Christ and to grow in His likeness!

Second, *Scripture provides instruction for knowing godliness.* Paul said that God-breathed Scripture was "profitable for doctrine" (2 Tim. 3:16), which refers to the comprehensive and complete body of divine truth. It is ridiculous to think that any person in our flock can know what godliness means without knowing biblical truth. Biblically ignorant people, even believers, are easy prey for the host of cults and false religions, many of whose teachers are easily accessible on television and radio everyday. Therefore, the diligent shepherd must engage his people in regular, systematic, and thorough teaching of the doctrine in God's inspired Word. And we can be confident that every bit of the wisdom and guidance for fulfilling everything God wants people to believe and do is found in it.

Third, *Scripture provides rebuke for straying from godliness.* The word "reproof" (v. 16) carries the idea of rebuking in order to convict of error in behavior or belief. This is necessary when people stray from the path of godly living. Through biblical preaching, shepherds can equip believers with accurate knowledge and understanding of divine truth. The faithful study and subsequent proclamation of God-breathed Scripture builds a foundation of truth that, among other things, penetrates people's lives with the intent of bringing correction, confession, renunciation, and obedience. Scripture precisely and thoroughly penetrates the believer's mind, soul, and heart. Beloved shepherd, reproving the wrongdoing of your people is as much your responsibility as building them up in righteousness. The inspired Scripture is the divine plumb line by which every thought, principle, act, and belief of your people is to be measured. God's Word is able to steer you and your flock away from sin and toward godliness.

Fourth, *Scripture provides restoration to godliness.* Paul calls this "correction" (v. 16). The word is found only here in the New Testament, and it refers to restoring something to its original and proper condition. After rebuking error in believers' lives, the shepherd must build them up with the divine correction of inspired Scripture. This is the Bible's way of making soothing, positive provision for those who have accepted the painful, negative reproof. Shepherd, your preaching of the Scriptures is God's primary channel for accomplishing this in the church.

Fifth, *Scripture provides training for pursuing godliness.* The translation "instruction" (v. 16) here is better rendered "training" or "discipline." In the present context it is best understood as the former in a broader and positive sense. The idea is that of instruction and building up. Teaching shepherds are God's instruments through which Scripture provides the training necessary for God's people to grow in Christlikeness. As we guide our people on regular journeys into God's inspired Word, "we all, with unveiled face, beholding as in a mirror the glory of the Lord, are being transformed into the same image from glory to glory, just as by the Spirit of the Lord" (2 Cor. 3:18).

Beloved shepherd, we cannot afford to lose sight of the foundational truth that the supreme source of power in our preaching is Holy Scripture. John MacArthur Jr. said, "Whether our purpose is to lead men and women to saving faith in Jesus Christ, to teach God's truth to believers, to refute error in the church, to correct and rebuild erring believers, or to train believers to live righteously, our supreme and sufficient resource is God's Word."[9] Accompanied with the transforming power of the Holy Spirit, Scripture is God's provision for every spiritual truth and moral principle that people need to be saved, equipped to live righteously in this life, and shaped into Christlikeness for the life to come. Of necessity then, shepherds must be totally committed to preaching, teaching, and obeying it. That is the only way we will glorify the God who gave it.

Changing the People

The Scripture not only equips the shepherd for his task, but it radically affects the people who hear and receive it. Have you ever thought about all of the incredible claims the Bible makes about its own spiritual power and ability to effect life change? Let me prompt your memory with just a few of the professions and promises Scripture makes about the potency it possesses to impact listeners in a lasting way. As we go along, notice the emphasis I have added to underscore some of the benefits to humanity that God's Word claims to give.

Joshua had to be just a little timid trying to fill the shoes of Moses after the death of the great deliverer. So God reminded him where his success rested by instructing him, "This Book of the Law shall not depart from your mouth, but you shall meditate in it day and night, that you may observe to do according to all that is written in it. For then you will make your way *prosperous,* and then you will have *good success"* (Josh. 1:8). Do you think *success* and *prosperity* are things people are interested in today?

The psalmist was all over the claims of Scripture regarding its ability to impact human nature. He said:

> The law of the LORD is perfect, *converting the soul;*
> The testimony of the LORD is sure, *making wise the simple;*
> The statutes of the LORD are right, *rejoicing the heart;*
> The commandment of the LORD is pure, *enlightening the eyes;*
> The fear of the LORD is clean, enduring forever;
> The judgments of the LORD are true and righteous altogether.
> More to be desired are they than gold,
> Yea, than much fine gold;
> Sweeter also than honey and the honeycomb.
> Moreover by them Your servant is *warned,*
> And in keeping them there is *great reward.*
> *Who can understand his errors?*
> *Cleanse me* from secret faults.
> *Keep back Your servant also from presumptuous sins;*
> Let them not have dominion over me.
> Then I shall be *blameless,*
> And I shall be innocent of great transgression (Ps. 19:7–13).

In this passage God's Word is referenced by six different titles—law, testimony, precepts, commandment, fear, and judgments. In those same verses, he mentions numerous characteristics of the Scriptures—perfect, sure, right, pure, clean, eternal, true, righteous, incredibly valuable, and very sweet! But be sure not to overlook all the blessings and benefits that God's Word brings—*restoration of the soul, wisdom, joy, understanding, warning, reward, conviction, cleansing, protection from sin,* and *blamelessness before God!* Our Lord has given us every truth, principle, standard, and warning that we will ever need for restoration into His image.

In chapter 119, that awesome discourse on the Word, the psalmist asked and answered:

> How can a young man *cleanse his way?*
> By taking heed according to Your word.
> With my whole heart I have sought You;

Oh, let me not wander from Your commandments!
Your word I have hidden in my heart,
That I might *not sin* against You (vv. 9–11).

Do you know anyone who needs *spiritual cleansing* or some help *preventing sin*? What about someone that could use a little awe-inspiring *wonder*? The psalmist cried,

Open my eyes, that I may see
Wondrous things from Your law (v. 18).

Or how about *direction for navigating life's journey*?

Your word is a *lamp to my feet*
And a *light to my path* (v. 105).

And imagine that—all without calling a 1-900 number to confide in a fortune-teller, tarot card reader, or other self-professed psychic!

The Old Testament prophets also knew the benefit of God's Word. Who can forget God's familiar words through Isaiah:

For as the rain comes down, and the snow from heaven,
And do not return there,
But *water* the earth,
And *make it bring forth and bud,*
That it may give *seed to the sower*
And *bread to the eater,*
So shall My word be that goes forth from My mouth;
It shall not return to Me void,
But it shall accomplish what I please,
And it shall *prosper* in the thing for which I sent it (55:10–11).

Oh, how our repentant sinners so often need a *heavenly drink* that enables them to *spiritually blossom* upon their return to God! Then they are able to receive the *grace-gifts* of His Word sowing and eating instead of being paralyzed by sorrow. All of this describes the *prosperity* that God brings!

And Jeremiah offered some encouragement for times when shepherds are staring into the solemn faces of parishioners, who reflect a desperate need for a good dose of *joy*! He excitedly announced,

Your words were found, and I ate them,
And Your word was to me the *joy and rejoicing of my heart*;

> For I am called by Your name,
> O LORD God of hosts (15:16).

The weeping prophet also conveyed God's own claim about His Word:

> "Is not My word like a fire?" says the LORD,
> "And like a hammer that *breaks the rock in pieces*?" (23:29).

The Scriptures are sufficient to confront hard hearts and difficult situations with *consuming* (implied) and *forceful* power!

The New Testament is also thick with claims about the awesome power of Scripture. We noted in the previous chapter the holy heartburn—or *heart change*—that took place in the disciples on the road to Emmaus after Jesus explained the Scriptures to them. They rhetorically asked, "Did not our *heart burn* within us while He talked with us on the road, and while He opened the Scriptures to us?" (Luke 24:32). Jesus Himself acknowledged the Word's role in *sanctification* when He prayed to the Father for His disciples: "*Sanctify* them by Your truth. Your word is truth" (John 17:17).

The apostle Paul got in on the action, too, recognizing the Scripture's power to foster *spiritual growth* and advancement toward *glorification* in the believer. He told the Ephesian elders, "Brethren, I commend you to God and to the word of His grace, which is able to *build you up* and *give you an inheritance among all those who are sanctified*" (Acts 20:32). To the Romans he said, "*Faith* comes by hearing, and hearing by the word of God" (Rom. 10:17), thus claiming God's Word as the originator of *faith*. He also called it "the sword of the Spirit" (Eph. 6:17), implying among other things its proactive and protective power of *conviction*.

Other New Testament writers followed suit. The author of Hebrews noted the Scripture's ability in *soul-searching* and *spiritual examination* when he claimed that "the word of God is living and powerful, and sharper than any two-edged sword, *piercing even to the division of soul and spirit, and of joints and marrow,* and is *a discerner of the thoughts and intents of the heart*" (4:12). And you do not even have to spend all that time and money on secular psychotherapy to figure yourself out! James spoke of the Word's ability to foster sanctifying wholeness when he told his readers to "lay aside all filthiness and overflow of wickedness, and receive with meekness the implanted word, which is able to *save your souls*" (1:21).

The apostle Peter spoke somewhat at length about the work of the Word. He said:

Since you have *purified your souls* in obeying the truth through
the Spirit in sincere love of the brethren, love one another fervently with a pure heart, having been *born again,* not of corruptible seed but incorruptible, through the word of God which
lives and abides forever, because

"All flesh is as grass,
And all the glory of man as the flower of the grass.
The grass withers,
And its flower falls away,
But the word of the LORD endures forever."

Now this is the word which by the gospel was preached to you.
Therefore, laying aside all malice, all deceit, hypocrisy, envy,
and all evil speaking, as newborn babes, desire the pure milk of
the word, that you may *grow* thereby (1 Pet. 1:22–2:2).

Have your run across anyone lately whose soul needs some *purity,* whose life
needs to be *born again,* or whose infant Christianity could just stand some
simple *spiritual nourishment*? The Scriptures can do all of that.

Now friend, listen. It's high time for the jury of Christian shepherds and
congregants to render a verdict. Either the Bible is true and all of these claims
are real, or the Bible is blowing smoke and we cannot trust it at any point. If we
assume that it is true and that all of these promises are certain, can you think of
anything more relevant for contemporary listeners? But here is the bigger question: Why would a shepherd want to give his flock anything else if, in fact, this is
where God has promised to invest His power? And why would the flock desire
to feed on anything else? If the Holy Spirit does all of this through God's Word
to effect life change, why would God's people feel the need to depend upon anything else to change them? Beloved, the shepherd's power in preaching is not in
his natural ability or personal skill but in the supernatural work of the Holy Spirit
through the Word. So it desperately needs to be loosed on the flock with complete confidence that it will do its re-creative and life-changing work!

The Work of the Spirit

When I sit around the breakfast table with my family every weekday morning,
I must admit that my kids do not look any different than they did the day
before. Oh, sometimes my daughter is wearing the exact same clothes she did

the previous day, and we have to send her back to the bedroom for retooling. But for all practical purposes they look pretty much like they did the previous day and even the previous week. But when I begin to mount the stairs after breakfast to finish getting ready for work, sometimes I find myself stopping to look at the family pictures that line the stairwell. And my thoughts are always the same, *Wow, my kids are growing up!*

Looking at them day by day at the breakfast table does not reveal any noticeable change. But comparing their yearly school pictures reveals a maturing process that often brings a small tear to the eye of a sentimental dad! The ironic thing about that scenario is that the daily breakfast table—along with our other eating events—is the very thing that enables the maturity that I am unable to notice day by day. As my wife prepares a steady diet of healthy meals, and those kids consume them, physical growth takes place. My kids are changing before my very eyes, without me even noticing!

In the same way, as shepherds serve up a steady diet of healthy Bible food and the flock consumes it, believers are being changed into the image of Christ. This is happening even though neither preacher nor people notice it on a week-by-week basis. It is the work of the Holy Spirit within them. Therefore, the effectiveness of pastoral preaching cannot and should not be gauged by what happens at the altar on Sunday morning or by what parishioners say as they shake the minister's hand at the back of the church after the service. The effectiveness of pastoral preaching must be gauged by whether or not we who listen to preaching look more like Jesus this year than we did this time last year. Here's how the Spirit works to bring about such change.

The Spirit and the Work of God

When I was a kid, I used to love watching *The Incredible Hulk* on television. It was the story of a scientist named David Banner whose body had accidentally been infused with some substance that made weird things happen. Every time he got mad or upset, his body went through a change in its physical form, also called *metamorphosis*. All of the sudden mild-mannered David Banner would turn into this incredibly large, green monster!

The Bible indicates that believers are going through a spiritual *metamorphosis* as they are being re-created into the "form" of Christ. As we have already determined, the Bible has one overarching theme from outset to conclusion—the redemption of God's creation. It opens in Genesis with the story of man's fall from the glorious image of God. It closes in Revelation with the ultimate restoration of that image in His eternal presence. Everything within the inspired inclusio describes God's plan of re-creation through Jesus Christ, a relationship with whom involves the process of *metamorphosis* into His likeness.

The New Testament describes this process as *transformation* into Christ's likeness and, in fact, uses the very word from which we get our word *metamorphosis*. Paul commanded the Romans not to be "conformed to this world, but be transformed [metamorphosis] by the renewing of your mind" (Rom. 12:2). Matthew also used the word to describe what happened to Jesus when He was *transfigured* in the presence of Peter, James, and John (see Matt. 17:2). His inner, divine nature and glory were made visible for a brief time. In like manner God desires the inner redeemed nature of every believer to be made visible in their daily living, as much as possible.

In one sense, believers have already been re-created into Christ's image. Paul told the Corinthians that "if anyone is in Christ, he is a new creation; old things have passed away; behold, all things have become new" (2 Cor. 5:17). But like so many concepts in Pauline theology, the re-creation of individuals into Christlikeness is a "now but not yet" reality (see Eph. 2:20–24; Col. 3:9–10). In other words, it is present in the believer's life, but it has to be appropriated and fleshed out. So while we have already been re-created spiritually, we are still being re-created practically through the constant working of the Holy Spirit.

Theology describes this entire process as the three-phased journey of salvation involving justification, sanctification, and glorification. It all leads to the glory of God! But notice that man's justification is inextricably linked to his glorification by the process of sanctification. This is the practical phase of the believer's development. While the possession of the new self brings the believer new life, it does not bring instant spiritual maturity. Throughout life, the flesh will continually tempt the new man to put on the garments of the old man. The new creation is complete, yet it has the capacity for growth, just as a baby is born complete yet still has the ability to grow: "Therefore we do not lose heart. Even though our outward man is perishing, yet the inward man is being renewed day by day" (2 Cor. 4:16).

This incredible metamorphosis of renewal actually manifests itself first in the human mind. Paul even said that believers are to be transformed "by the renewing of your mind" (Rom. 12:2), indicating that the outward change is effected by an inner change in the mind. As Christ is formed in the believer, His Spirit works to transform our thinking. This is the same thing Paul was talking about when he said our new man was "renewed in knowledge according to the image of Him who created him" (Col. 3:10). The language here indicates that this is a new quality of life that never existed before. Our depraved mind, which was part of the old man, was in constant decay. But in Christ, the mind of the new man is continually being renewed. So when the apostle said, "Let this mind be in you which was also in Christ Jesus," (Phil. 2:5), he really meant it!

This Holy Spirit's work of metamorphosis will not be fully realized in believers until the completion of the divine agenda. The concept is far too incredible for even the sanctified mind to comprehend. The New Testament, however, does provide us with some hint of what we ultimately will look like.[10]

First, we will be like Christ *spiritually*. Although this does not mean we will become deity, it is the more lofty and weighty of the two kinds of likeness. These corruptible bodies that we have now will be traded in for incorruptible bodies, and we will be permeated with the very holiness of Christ. Then we will be perfect both outwardly and inwardly, just like Jesus.

Second, we will be like Christ *bodily*. Paul told the Philippians that one day Christ Jesus "will transform our lowly body that it may be conformed to His glorious body, according to the working by which He is able even to subdue all things to Himself" (Phil. 3:21). So, just "as we have borne the image of the man of dust, we shall also bear the image of the heavenly Man" (1 Cor. 15:49).

In the meantime, God's Holy Spirit is working to make every believer progressively more and more like the Lord Jesus Christ who created us. It is God's plan to re-create believers to be like Jesus Christ, "for whom He foreknew, He also predestined to be conformed to the image of His Son, that He might be the firstborn among many brethren" (Rom. 8:29). Our new man will continue to progress toward Christlikeness until Jesus returns or our physical body dies. Beloved, until then we have this hope, that "now we are children of God; and it has not yet been revealed what we shall be, but we know that when He is revealed, we shall be like Him, for we shall see Him as He is" (1 John 3:2).

The Spirit and the Word of God

But what does all of this have to do with the shepherd and those he feeds? The work of divine metamorphosis in the believer's life is directly linked to the application of the Word of God by the Holy Spirit. Scripture instructs us to allow ourselves to be transformed on the outside in keeping with what is on the inside (see Rom. 12:2). That is why Paul assured the Corinthians that "we all, with unveiled face, beholding as in a mirror the glory of the Lord, are being transformed into the same image from glory to glory, just as by the Spirit of the Lord" (2 Cor. 3:18). Although we can and should desire to be transformed, we must understand that it only happens as the Holy Spirit renews our minds with God's Word.

Therein is the link between the preaching event and metamorphosis into Christlikeness. This practical phase of the believer's re-creation is the aspect of salvation to which the teaching shepherd is most notably assigned. And the primary tool which has been given to him for such a task is none other than God's supernatural Word. When Jesus prayed passionately for His flock which was soon to be scattered, He cried out to His Father, "Sanctify them by Your truth. Your word is truth" (John 17:17). The primary agent the Holy Spirit uses to transform believers into Christ's image is the very Word that reveals this divine agenda—the Bible!

It is through spiritual transformation that God glorifies Himself in the preaching event. Our ultimate conformity to Christ—glorification—will be God's gracious adornment of His children with the very glory of His Son, Jesus Christ! As our preaching is driven by a passion for God's glory, He uses His Word to transform individuals in the likeness of Christ by clothing them in His glory (see 2 Cor. 3:18; Phil. 3:21; Heb. 1:2–3). This makes these two kinds of likeness to Christ interrelated as part of a continuum. Right now in this world we are in the process of being transformed into Christlikeness. Through the truth of God's Word, we are being made to look more and more like Jesus, headed for the time when we will look exactly like Him in body and spirit. Someone has rightly said that we ought to be looking so much more like Jesus every day that only a slight change should be necessary when we finally see Him!

This is why the apostle Paul devoted himself to realizing this transformation of believers into the divine image through the preaching and teaching of God's Word. He knew that Scripture was God's primary agent for divine transformation, reflected in his claim that we all look at God's glory as we look into the mirror of His Word, and as a result we are being transformed into His same image from glory to glory (see 2 Cor. 3:18). Like James, Paul used a mirror as an analogy for the supernatural, truth-telling Scriptures (see James 1:23–25). His ministry of God's Word was driven by a desire to see men and women once again reflect the image in which they had originally been created.

The apostle's labor in preaching also helps us to understand the connection between God's agenda of re-creation and the ultimate passion for God's glory. Knowing that Jesus Christ "will transform our lowly body that it may be *conformed to His glorious body*" (Phil. 3:21, emphasis added), he told the Colossians:

> To them God willed to make known what are the riches of the
> glory of this mystery among the Gentiles: which is *Christ in
> you, the hope of glory.* Him we preach, warning every man and
> teaching every man in all wisdom, that we may present every
> man perfect in Christ Jesus. To this end I also labor, striving
> according to His working which works in me mightily
> (Col. 1:27–29, emphasis added).

Paul understood that the re-creation of mankind into the divine image was fostered by God's Word, and consequently it would result in God's glory as His creatures once again reflected His glorious nature!

The apostle Peter clarified even further the relationship between re-creation, preaching, and God's glory by also identifying God's words as the primary agent of transformation. He said that "divine power has given to us all things that pertain to life and godliness, through the knowledge of Him who called us by glory and virtue, by which have been given to us *exceedingly great and precious promises,* that through these you may be partakers of *the divine nature*" (2 Pet. 1:3–4, emphasis added). God calls us to reflect His glory and virtue through a relationship with Jesus Christ. His Word contains everything that we need for gaining that knowledge. Furthermore, that knowledge is possible because we have inherited the divine nature which is fleshed out in godly living. In other words, God has given us through His Word everything we need in order to know Him and be transformed into His nature!

If the shepherd is going to preach for the glory of God, he will have to do it in keeping with God's agenda, which is dictated by the essence of His Word. So both preacher and people must simply let the Bible be what it was intended to be and do what it was intended to do—transform us into the image of Jesus Christ. Nothing more, nothing less.

Where Do I Go from Here...

Now that you have come to this place in the philosophy of shepherding, you may proceed one of two ways as indicated by the shaded areas on the chart below. The (▼) symbol indicates the thematic development of more of these philosophical considerations. If you are following this path, proceed to chapter 6, "The Shepherd's Relevance." The (➡) symbol indicates the continued development of the *resource* for preaching from these beginning philosophical considerations on to their practical implications. If you are following this path, proceed to chapter 8, "Preaching with Potency." Before beginning chapter 8, however, be sure to read the introduction to part 3, "Passion-Driven Sermonology."

Table 5.1

	PART 1 (Biblical)		PART 2 (Philosophical)		PART 3 (Practical)
(Content)	Chapter 1: The Message of Preaching ▼	➡	Chapter 4: The Shepherd's Stewardship ▼	➡	Chapter 7: Preaching as Worship ▼
(Resource)	Chapter 2: The Means for Preaching ▼	➡	Chapter 5: The Shepherd's Power ▼	➡	Chapter 8: Preaching with Potency ▼
(Goal)	Chapter 3: The Motive in Preaching	➡	Chapter 6: The Shepherd's Relevance	➡	Chapter 9: Preaching for Eternity

CHAPTER 6

The Shepherd's Relevance:
APPLICATION OR INCARNATION?

"More heresy is preached in application than in Bible exegesis."[1] Those are the words of Haddon Robinson, one of the most notable preachers and professors of preaching in our day. He was bemoaning the disconnect that exists in much preaching between the truth of the biblical text and the application that is made to the listeners. While Robinson's words were never more true than they are today, I wonder if the "heresy" that's being preached in the contemporary pulpit is not of an even more subtle nature. Maybe the commentary on preaching in our day simply ought to be, "More application is preached than Bible exegesis." My addition of Robinson's statement is simply intended to call attention to the modern-day worship of the functional element of application by many preachers, as well as by many of those who listen to them preach. It appears that this important aspect of preaching has become the god of the modern Sunday morning sermon event. And such allegiance has caused application to take on a life of its own.

As many shepherds pay homage to the idols of felt needs, seeker-sensitivity, and western individualism, the concept of application has evolved into a perverted albatross. This perversion has distracted and even paralyzed many of God's shepherds from moving their people toward faith development. While preaching may have once erred on the side of weighty exegesis with no connection to the real world, its contemporary crime is in reverse. Today, application is the sermon and exegesis is the servant. This tragic reversal, which short-circuits preaching's supernatural power, beckons us to reconsider the issue. Actually, what's needed is for Christian preachers and listeners to reform this element from the humanism that invaded the pulpit in the last century.

Reforming Application from the Outside In

In the preface to his outstanding book entitled *The Supremacy of God in Preaching*, John Piper tells about a time when he decided to test whether or not the lofty subject of the greatness of God would in and of itself meet the needs of people. In a particular Sunday sermon, he unfolded the vision of God's holiness recorded in Isaiah 6:1–4 without giving one word of application! Piper described what happened:

> I didn't realize that not long before this Sunday one of the young families of our church discovered that their child was being sexually abused by a close relative. It was incredibly traumatic. They were there that Sunday morning and sat under that message. I wonder how many advisers to us pastors today would have said: "Pastor Piper, can't you see your people are hurting? Can't you come down out of the heavens and get practical? Don't you realize what kind of people sit in front of you on Sunday?" Some weeks later I learned the story. The husband took me aside one Sunday after service. "John," he said, "these have been the hardest months of our lives. Do you know what has gotten me through? The vision of the greatness of God's holiness that you gave me the first week of January. It has been the rock we could stand on."[2]

Piper confirmed that themes like God's greatness, holiness, and glory *are* pertinent to the lives of people, even if they do not show up on surveys listing the felt needs of our listeners. There is a hidden cry in every human soul to know the glory of God!

In light of the modern infatuation with application, the concept desperately needs some reformation. We must begin by looking outside at its basic nature so that we can then work inward to a healthy understanding of its focus. To do this we will once again need to view it through the biblical lense of re-creation into the image of Jesus Christ in the lives of His people. Application must be defined according to the agenda of God in Scripture.

Reclaiming the Relevance

Application in preaching is actually driven by the deeper issue of relevance or the relationship between the truth of God's Word and those who listen to it. Application is merely the vehicle for establishing that relationship. Relevance suggests that something is pertinent to someone, and that "something" possesses the ability to retrieve material that satisfies that person's needs. While relevance is practical, it possesses an especially social applicability. So relevance involves not only how we act but how we relate. Application, then, is not primarily about addressing perceived needs with practical advice but addressing *real* needs and restoring *right* relationships.

One of the great needs of contemporary preaching is for shepherds to reclaim a more mature, holistic understanding of the nature of relevance. Today, discussions about relevance in preaching are almost without exception limited to the *concrete*. We refer to the practical instruction that sermons offer listeners and the practical demands they make upon them. But what about the *abstract* relevance of biblical truth? While the Bible certainly contains many practical truths and implications thereof regarding various aspects of human existence, it concerns itself primarily with matters that are more utopian, visionary, speculative, and undemonstrable.

In the Old Testament, for example, the Bible speaks of man being created in the image of God, in His likeness. Like Abraham, God's people are told to live in this world according to the promise of another world. They are called to be perfect just as He is perfect. They are to be holy as God is holy, and they are to reflect His glory.

In the New Testament, Jesus' followers are summoned to the crucified life where they are to die to self daily. It's not the disciple who lives but Christ who lives in the disciple. And the physical life of the disciple is lived by faith in the crucified Christ. At the same time, Christians are told they are incapable of living the Christ life just as they were incapable of saving themselves. Yet they are told to walk in the Spirit and not in the flesh, by faith and not by sight. And while they are children of God in this world, it is yet to be revealed what they will look like in the next. But it is according to the next world that they are to live in the present one. These ideas are conceptual and notional. They are more relational and less practical. To say the least, they sometimes are hard to get our arms around, much less to know "how to" do them!

That doesn't mean these truths of God's Word are irrelevant, however. In fact, they are foundational for human existence as well as Christian service. It's interesting to notice how, as with Piper's parishioner, the lofty concepts of the faith seem to motivate and inspire us more than the concrete principles. They become the firm foundation on which we are able to navigate all the stuff this life throws at us. Take this younger generation of Christ's followers as another example. They are not the least motivated by Christian denominations, agencies, and institutions. But give them a vision of the greatness of a global God who is on an unstoppable mission in this world, and they will sacrifice everything!

As a seminary professor, I have noticed two interesting qualities that characterize many of the students we have today. First, they love to study theology. They love to learn about the nature of God and the great doctrines that flow from His being. Second, they are not impressed with the things that impressed me when I was a student. I remember being willing to stand in line or drive a hundred miles to hear the preaching of the "big guns" who pastored the megachurches. Yet even some of the students today who have the potential of being those high-profile leaders of tomorrow would just as soon plant their lives in an inner-city project somewhere and infiltrate it with the gospel. I think there may be a relationship between those two characteristics. Being caught up in the greatness and sovereignty of God has a way of moving people to God-sized tasks!

Relevance, however, is determined not only by the broader purpose of preaching for God's glory but also by the specific purpose of each preaching event. And every serious student of preaching knows that the purpose of each individual message should be to secure some moral action, not simply to communicate doctrine as an end unto itself. A. W. Tozer reminded us that

> there is scarcely anything so dull and meaningless as Bible doctrine taught for its own sake. Truth divorced from life is not truth in its Biblical sense, but something else and something less. . . . Theological truth is useless until it is obeyed.[3]

If the proclamation of the glory of God truly is relevant for modern man, then its implications must be obeyed by those who behold it!

But how do we go about determining the purpose of an individual message, a purpose that both glorifies God and can be obeyed by the listeners. The only way is simply to allow the inspired author's purpose to determine the contemporary preacher's purpose. The apostle Paul told young Timothy that the purpose of every passage of Scripture was "that the man of God may be complete, thoroughly equipped for every good work" (2 Tim. 3:17). Notice the means by which Paul said that would be accomplished—*doctrine, reproof, correction,* and *instruction* (see 2 Tim. 3:16). If we are to be relevant in contemporary preaching, the purposes of our sermons must line up with these means, the only means by which real-life change occurs!

As we determined in the previous chapter, only the last of these four means implies something the listener actually *does*! This suggests that obedience and subsequent life change are not necessarily limited to the listener's practical and physical response. Obedience may be demonstrated as the listener embraces the preacher's exhortation to both cognitive and affective responses. Haddon Robinson said that the preacher "should be able to put into words what beliefs, attitudes, or values should change or be confirmed, or what quality of life or what good works should result from the preaching and hearing of [his] sermon."[4]

According to Paul, the man of God can accomplish preaching's purpose by (1) teaching a doctrine, (2) refuting some error, belief, or action, (3) correcting something that is wrong, and (4) giving people instruction for navigating life. This is why homileticians through the years have championed for less action-oriented objectives (teaching doctrine, providing knowledge and information, offering support and comfort, inspiring devotion, and changing attitudes) along with the more action-oriented objectives (consecration, ethical improvement, challenge, and skill development).[5]

Relevance in preaching must be defined and determined, not by the perspective of the preacher or the listeners, but by the nature of God and His Word. And if God's agenda is to bring glory and honor to His name by re-creating individuals into His likeness, then such is relevance in the preaching event. When shepherds proclaim the Bible in keeping with its purpose and power, then relevance is a reality.

Redefining the Meaning

Not only do we need to reclaim relevance as determined by God's Word and God's nature, but we desperately need to redefine the meaning of application in the preaching event. The bottom line is that we need to broaden our understanding of it. My only disagreement with Piper about his Isaiah 6 sermon is that I think he *did* do application, at least in the larger way it ought to be understood. He exposed the revelation of God about Himself, which obviously helped to form godliness in a hurting father, thus enabling him to victoriously navigate life's garbage dump. Actually that is re-creation, which is far more valuable to contemporary listeners than the shallow application they are being served in many pulpits today!

Application, by definition, is basically the act of putting to use. Like relevance, it most often speaks of the practical value of a thing. We think of application as linking the importance of the truth of a text with the hearer's situation and need by not only leading them to accept what has been stated but to act upon its counsel. It is the way preachers involve the listeners in the sermon.

Today application in preaching most often involves showing listeners how-to live out particular Bible truths, how to know God, how specific problems can be solved, how to grow spiritually, how to perform Christian service, or how-to live a better life. The operative terms, of course, are *practical* and *how to*. And if something is "practical" then we most often think it demands a how-to.

A good example of this is going to the doctor. If I go to the doctor when I have the flu, he gives me some antibiotics. I go home and take the medication according to the prescription. In other words, I apply the medicine. The medication battles the flu bug in my body, and sooner or later I get well. That is practical. I am doing something that someone prescribed in order to address a problem in my life. The doctor prescribes something that is relevant for my life, and I go home and apply it.

As we implied above, however, application doesn't always have to be aggressive in order to be fleshed out. I don't always have to take some physical action in order for God's truth to be obeyed and put to use in my life. Application can be passive in some instances. Someone else can apply something to my life and it still have practical value as long as I embrace it by faith. As I embrace God's truth by faith, it takes root in my life and produces practical benefit without my ever *doing* anything other than receiving it.

If I go to the same doctor for a routine physical, he might suggest in the course of his examination that I get a flu shot to prepare for the upcoming flu season. Practicality, as it is being used in preaching today, would suggest that it is ridiculous for me to get the shot. After all, isn't the shot irrelevant for my life since I do not have the flu? No, my analysis is the thing that is ridiculous. Of course I should get the shot, then go home and proceed about my business. The shot works to prevent my body from ever hosting the flu bug. That does not appear to be practical since I'm not doing anything, but I would submit to you that practical value has still been applied to my life because I had faith enough to get the shot.

Another related issue that will help us to navigate the muddy waters of application is to understand the distinctions between various kinds of application. For example, *specific application* is the linking of truth with a current situation in the listener's life. On the other hand, *stored application* involves truth that is being deposited and kept for life situations and circumstances that the listener has not yet begun to even fathom. In both cases application is being made to the listener's life. While most listeners only perceive *specific application* to be relevant, they must also understand that *stored application* is equally relevant, and maybe even more so.

Imagine if we built our educational systems on *specific application*. In other words, what if we taught students in educational settings only the material that they could use at that particular stage in their lives? To be sure, we would never teach much. When students attend school, very little of what they are taught is specifically applied to their lives at the time they are learning it. Most of it is *stored application*. Information that they will need in various life situations is being logged into their minds. Students at all levels often complain and say, "This is a waste of time; I'll never use this!" The wise teacher or parent knows better.

Yet there is still a third type of application that is overlooked even more than *stored application*. *Subliminal application* is application that is made below the threshold of consciousness. During the late 1970s and early 1980s, there was a big concern that some record companies and recording artists were putting suggestive, subliminal messages on record albums. Backward masking was the big scare. Supposedly the messages were inaudible, yet in bypassing the hearing they were able to enter the unconscious mind. I am told the same thing can happen visually when movie frames picturing popcorn and soft drinks are inserted in a movie reel at a theater, undetectable to the naked eye. Yet the subliminal images allegedly can prompt hunger and thirst in the minds of the clueless viewer. I don't completely understand how all of this works, but I do find it interesting that information can be applied to a human life without being detected in the consciousness.

If this can happen with the natural man, why is it so hard for us to fathom its occurrence in the spiritual man who has both mental and spiritual capacities? As God's supernatural truth is deposited in the hearts and minds of His people, their minds are transformed and their spirits are nourished without them ever being aware of the dynamics of the process. There is a spiritual magnetism between the Spirit who indwells the believer and the Word He inspired. In stealth fashion, then, the believer's re-created nature is being fleshed out. Much the same thing happens physically when human beings eat. We all take food into our bodies, but few of us are conscious of how and when the body breaks down the food and manipulates it in order to provide nourishment and make us healthy.

I am not at all trying to negate what we said in chapter 4 about the necessity of understanding truth with the mind. Neither am I suggesting that *subliminal application* be the only type on which preacher and people rely. Certainly all three kinds of application demand some degree of comprehension with the mind in order for truth to find its way into the heart. Teaching shepherds and their listeners need to understand, however, that God's supernatural truth can find a nesting place in our hearts even when we are not completely cognizant of every aspect of the process. While truth applied subliminally still has to go through the mind of the listener, it may not necessarily be analyzed to the same degree as the other kinds of application.

It has been suggested that unless listeners remember everything the preacher says, there can be no application or subsequent life change. While I believe preachers should do everything within their power to assist listeners in remembering their sermons, I beg to differ with the contention that all of the Word's effectualness is negated when memory loses its grasp. Over the past twenty years of marriage, I estimate that I have eaten far more than six thousand wonderful meals my wife has prepared. And yet I would be hard pressed to recite to you the menus, much less the ingredients, of any of them other than maybe a couple from the last week. But I can say with great certainty that had I not consumed them, I would be dead today! Similarly, we can be sure that some degree of supernatural nourishment is taking place every time God's Word is rightly preached, even if total analysis and retention are absent.

Redeeming the Focus

So what does all this mean for the shepherd who desires to speak relevantly to the hearts and lives of his people? Just this—that his most relevant preaching is that which connects the truth of God's Word with the greatest needs of the most number of people. Consequently, the shepherd will need to redeem application from the haphazard and limited role to which it has been reduced in much contemporary preaching, and once again focus it on that which glorifies God. This kind of preaching stewardship demands that we ask an important question: *What approach to application provides the preacher with the best chance of connecting eternal truth with the most number of listeners?*

To answer this question, picture the application process as a funnel, with the widest area of passage being at the top and the smallest being at the bottom (see Figure 1). A funnel actually serves as a medium for catching and directing a downward flow into a specific place, like gasoline being put into a lawn mower. In addition to providing direction, the proper use of the funnel prevents the least amount of the substance from being lost in the process. For it to work, however, the substance must be poured into the wide end, not the narrow end. The design of the funnel naturally directs the flow into the narrower areas.

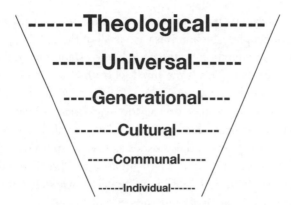

Figure 1: The Application Funnel

It seems that many modern pulpiteers have all but reversed the natural application of God's Word. By giving all of their attention in application to selected groups and individual listeners, they are investing precious time and energy in areas where they have the least chance of connecting with the most people. And worse, the truth of God's Word often is spilled out and lost in the process!

As Figure 1 indicates, application should be viewed as the process of focusing eternal truth into the hearts and minds of individual listeners. In order for that to happen, however, the preacher must intentionally pour—or apply—God's Word into the areas that connect with the most number of people. That's the only way he ultimately will be able to make specific application to individual lives with any degree of integrity. Let me suggest six considerations wherein the preacher can establish a logical, significant relationship between biblical truth and the largest number of his listeners without losing substance along the way. Like the funnel, these considerations are mentioned in decreasing order of priority, each one being a subgroup of the one that precedes it.

The shepherd's first thought in establishing relevance should be given to *theological application.* This is application that answers the question, "What does the given biblical text teach us about God and His relationship with people?" If application is, in fact, about addressing real needs and restoring right relationships, then its widest and most important connecting point is with that part of mankind which relates to the Creator. Every listener who comes to any preaching event possesses the ultimate need to know God and live in relation to Him. Consequently, preaching that seeks to exalt the person of God and the ensuing implications for humanity is the most relevant preaching for the most number of people, which in this case is all of them!

The second consideration for the preacher in establishing relevance should be *universal application.* This is the timeless truth in any given passage that is applicable to all people of all time. The Christian shepherd can be confident that the Bible addresses in some way all the major issues of life—human identity, the reason for existence, the future, guilt, love, significance, death, eternity, and more. Scripture speaks to these issues as they relate to the redemption of mankind and the transformation of individuals into Christlikeness. What God has to say to all people of all time is foundational for what He has to say to individuals in a particular time, including the present.

The preacher's attention then should naturally turn to *generational application.* Here the shepherd addresses that which is constant for all people living on planet earth at the time the message is preached. By *generation* I mean the group of individuals born and living contemporaneously. There are always certain qualities that characterize every living generation and distinguish it from the preceding and succeeding ones. Whenever the shepherd seeks to connect the Word of God with characteristics of his generation, he is sure to strike a chord of relevance with all of his listeners.

The next consideration must be given to *cultural application,* that which connects the Scriptures to things germane to all people within a particular culture. As the funnel of relevance narrows, the preacher's chance of connecting with every listener decreases, making application more difficult. So he must allow the flow to be natural, not forcing application beyond what Scripture allows. The plethora of customary beliefs, social forms, and material traits of various countries, races, people groups, and other social and religious entities certainly presents an interesting challenge for any preacher in our current global melting pot. The conscientious shepherd must seek to connect eternal truth with the sets of shared attitudes, values, goals, and practices that characterize the culture or cultures in his immediate context. Then he can be confident that he is establishing relevance with most of his listeners.

The fifth consideration for the preacher in establishing relevance in the minds of his listeners is *communal application.* This involves the connection of biblical truth with those persons whose lives are bonded together by some type of common relationship. This may be manifested in families, close-knit communities, same occupations, shared life situations, similar struggles, or some other characteristic which groups of individuals have in common. This level of application is even more difficult than the previous one, however, because not everyone who comes to church will have a common tie to any of the numerous other groups within the congregation. To be sure, most public worship services will be made up of a combination of "insiders" and "outsiders." As the shepherd attempts to address subjects germane to one particular communal entity, he will always find himself of necessity missing a number of his listeners.

The most limited consideration for the preacher—and yet the one that gets the most attention in our day—is *individual application*. This, of course, is when the preacher seeks to identify and address the needs of individual listeners or selected groups. While this kind of application usually is of the most interest to listeners, it is inevitably the most limited in the larger scope of things. The more individualized and specific the preacher becomes, the fewer number of people he is likely to address, and the less relevant his preaching becomes with regard to the purpose of preaching and the agenda of the Almighty. Additionally, if the preacher ventures to this area without first passing through the other considerations, he likely will find himself making God say some things He never said! Thus, Robinson's words become prophetic: *More heresy is preached in application than in Bible exegesis!*

Most preachers spend their time trying to apply biblical truth in these last three areas—cultural, communal, and individual—all of which run higher risks of ignoring significant groups of people. And most of the time, caring and empathetic shepherds start from the bottom up! They get so consumed with making specific application to individuals that they never consider the degree to which their preaching relates to the larger congregation. Both preachers and listeners must acknowledge the myth that suggests preaching is irrelevant if it fails to make specific application to each individual listener. Why? Because a whole lot of application is germane to each individual listener as part of creation and humanity, as well as part of a particular generation, culture, and community.

None of this is to say that the preacher should not be concerned with specific application to the lives of his individual listeners. Certainly, every preacher must give serious attention to whom he will be speaking and how he might establish relevancy in each heart and mind. John the Baptist, Jesus, Paul, and the other apostles were concerned that people acted rightly based on specific application of truth (e.g., Matt. 7:21–27; Luke 3:10–14; Eph. 4:25–32; James 2:14–26). But they provided such application only after allowing it to flow naturally from a consideration of broader theological ideas. About Paul's letters, Thompson observed that all of them move toward a call for a change of conduct among the listeners supported with careful theological argumentation. The ethical exhortations, which are most often (but not always) found near the end of the Pauline letter, are not to be regarded as the appendix to a theological treatise, but rather as the climax of the argument in which theological argument provides the basis for change.[6]

Such is an important model for contemporary preaching. And the shepherd has a lot better chance of being relevant to the largest number of people when he focuses on the broader considerations and works through them toward specific application to individuals and selected groups.

Transforming Lives from the Inside Out

As the Word of God is applied to the lives of believers through the application funnel, they essentially are being conformed to Christ's image (see Rom. 8:29; Phil. 3:10,21). To say it another way, He is *formed* inside them. Essentially, that makes the salvation of human beings the second "incarnation." Incarnation simply is the embodiment of deity in some earthly form. The first incarnation was when the Son of God "became flesh and dwelt among us, and we beheld His glory, the glory as of the only begotten of the Father" (John 1:14). The second incarnation, as Paul told the Colossians, is "Christ in you, the hope of glory" (Col. 1:27). When a person comes to Christ, deity takes up residence. And Christ incarnate in the believer is the hope of glory!

While preaching is always directed at the whole man, both preachers and listeners must understand that transformation occurs from the inside out, not the other way around. It is helpful to think of listeners as being multidimensional, having both a material and an immaterial nature. When a person is born again, he or she receives an additional component—the character of Christ as revealed through the Holy Spirit—and becomes a part of the faith community (see Figure 2). An awareness of the interrelationship of these parts tells us much about how and why we do what we do. Also, it says a whole lot about how incarnational preaching fosters life change.

Preaching for Christ's Character

The initial target of incarnational preaching is the very center of the listener's being, the character of Christ within (see Figure 2). This is not to say that the shepherd is preaching to Christ but preaching to nurture the character of

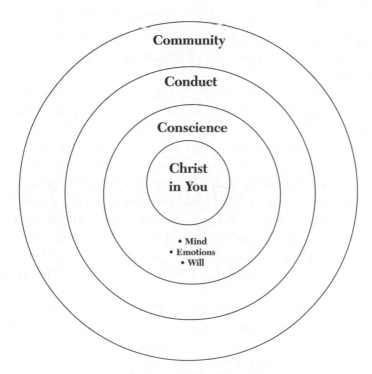

Figure 2: Incarnational Preaching

Christ within the believer. The character of Christ as revealed through the Holy Spirit is the primary influence on how the believer thinks, feels, and desires. The way we think, feel, and desire, then, determines how we act. And how we act as individuals affects the way we live in community.

Such an understanding stands in direct opposition to the world's mind-set. In general, people think the way you affect the body is by working from the outside in. We think that changing our physical circumstances will determine how we think and feel. So we work on communication skills in order to get along better with family members without first growing in love, the first fruit of the Spirit. We change jobs in order to be happy before we mature our joy, a fruit of the Spirit which defies outward circumstances. We diet to control our weight instead of first developing self-control to guide our eating habits. And so on.

The real tragedy in this irony is that contemporary preaching has fallen prey to its deception. Many shepherds preach sermons that feed this perversion. Our bent toward pragmatism leads us to think that if we just align our bodies—our behavior—with certain principles and actions, then life-change will occur. So we gravitate toward life-application messages loaded with supposed practical principles. And then we go home Sunday after Sunday with a grocery bag full of *good stuff* that will change our lives from the outside in. Or will it?

The spiritual makeup of man actually suggests the other way around. Paul said to "work out your own salvation with fear and trembling; for it is God who works in you both to will and to do for His good pleasure" (Phil. 2:12–13). Obviously he was not instructing us to make arrangements for our own salvation. He was telling us to work it out from within, to make sure what is on the inside shows up on the outside! This is how you make salvation operational. The justification part has to be followed by the experiential aspects of sanctification where the new character of Christ is consciously appropriated and demonstrated (see Gal. 5:22–23). And notice that the enablement to carry out this process is furnished by God Himself. He is the one who gives the believer both the desire to live righteously and the effective energy to do so. That means He gets the glory!

What does all this say about the shepherd's preaching? Simply this, that his primary and initial target ought to be the spiritual force within his listeners, not their behavior. Again, therein is the vanity of trying to "principlize" the Bible and preach on every detail of daily living. According to an old proverb, "If you give a man a fish, you feed him for a day. But if you teach a man to fish, you feed him for a lifetime." God knew that. So instead of giving His children a manual full of instructions for navigating every single detail of daily life, He deposited in them the source of infinite wisdom and knowledge, the character of the Lord Jesus. And it is the Holy Spirit whom Christ has given to apply the wisdom and knowledge of truth to the infinite number of variables in everyday life experiences (see Luke 11:9–13; John 16:8–11; James 1:2–8).

Consequently, shepherds need to feed the character of Christ within their listeners with spiritual food. The goal of every pastoral sermon first and foremost needs to be to "fatten" that new character within each person who listens so that He gradually takes over the mind, will, and emotions, and then ultimately the actions. And the character of Christ feeds off the Word of God. So shepherds again can be free to teach and preach the Bible in keeping with the intended meaning of His Spirit who inspired it. And listeners can be confident that the character of Christ within them is being nourished with supernatural food, for the Spirit of Christ who indwells every believer gravitates toward the very words He has given.

Preaching for Christ's Conscience

My waistline often reminds me that the age-old proverb "You are what you eat" is true when it comes to the physical man. My Bible, however, tells me something completely different when it comes to the spiritual man. One of the God-inspired proverbs says that a man is what he *thinks,* not what he eats (see Prov. 23:7). That means convictions, mind-sets, and worldviews play a crucial role in determining who we are and how we act.

Consequently, the shepherd's second concern in his preaching is still not to alter his listeners' conduct but to alter their consciences. The conscience is the true center of human personality, combining a sense of the moral goodness or blameworthiness of one's own conduct, intentions, or character with a feeling of obligation to do right or be good. In psychoanalysis, it is the part of the super-ego that transmits commands and admonitions to the ego. Very simply, the conscience is the seat of the mind, will, and emotions (see Figure 2). It is the link between our inner man and our outer man, enabling us to relate to the physical world through the body and to God through the Spirit.

As the character of Christ within the listener is fed, incarnational preaching naturally begins to speak to the souls of people as they grow into the image of Christ. Shepherds need to be concerned with the way people think and feel before they worry about the way they act. As the Spirit of God within an individual grows more influential, He begins to affect the person's conscience (see Figure 2). It is far more important for the shepherd to teach people to "think Christianly" than to act rightly. Acting rightly will only help them in the immediate and the specific situation. Thinking Christianly will enable them to view every situation in life with the mind of Christ, even those situations which neither the preacher nor the listener has yet to fathom.

If I were given a choice in preaching between affecting a listener's conscience and affecting his or her conduct, I would choose to affect the conscience. The issue of conduct is specific and narrow, limited to a particular situation or circumstance. Conscience, on the other hand, is general and broad, influencing any number of varying life situations. A person's convictions and standards—what they believe—apply to the multiplicity of issues that he or she will face along life's path. Preaching to change conduct, as it is being fleshed out in the pragmatic preaching of our day, primarily makes a one-to-one connection between the sermon and a particular problem or situation. A person needs help raising teenagers, so the shepherd delivers a how-to or "principle" sermon on the subject. The content of the message is limited to the situation. A sermon on the character and nature of the heavenly Father, however, has relevance for the current parental problem as well as a host of other life issues that beg for a divine familial perspective.

Thinking Christianly means looking at every situation in life through the eyes of the Lord Jesus and analyzing them according to His mind. The apostle Paul said, "Let this mind be in you which was also in Christ Jesus" (Phil. 2:5). In essence, that means forming a Christian worldview. Worldview is basically the grid through which a person looks at the world based on what he or she considers to be the truth. It encompasses how people perceive themselves, others, and ultimately God.[7] The importance of worldview cannot be underestimated. Pastoral preaching must seek to form the mind of Christ in the conscience of every believer.

Preaching for Christ's Conduct

As Christ's character is formed in the listener through biblical preaching, and as His character begins to influence the listener's conscience, only then is conduct genuinely affected. Then and only then does the shepherd begin to shape human conduct according to the conduct of Christ (see Figure 2). As people begin to think Christianly, they will begin to decide for Christ in every aspect of life, for faith is always expressed in the willful obedience to God's Word. Incarnational preaching is fleshed out in Christian conduct.

The preaching event is fueled by the desire to see people respond positively to God's Word in such a way that it affects their conduct. Daniel J. Baumann said that preaching is "the communication of biblical truth by man to men with the explicit purpose of eliciting behavioral change."[8] Building upon the intellectual and emotional change of the conscience, this definition magnifies the implicit call in the preaching event for a faith response that informs daily conduct. Part of the purpose of preaching, then, ought to be to see faith expressed in the conduct as a result of character formation and conscience alteration.

Let me give you an example of how all this works. One of the movements God has used in curbing the escalation of premarital sex among teenagers is the True Love Waits campaign. Thousands of teens have made noble commitments to abstain from sex until they are married. But many of them have made such commitments in the midst of great frustration because they weren't helped to know how conduct is genuinely shaped. Do you know how frustrating it is for teenagers to be told, "Don't have sex until you're married," when their bodies are telling them just the opposite! True love won't necessarily wait just because a parent says it should or even because a youth worker offers some practical ways to avoid compromising situations. The only way a teenager can say no to such a natural drive is through self-control. And self-control is part of the fruit of the Spirit, the very character of Christ. As that character is nurtured through biblical teaching, firm convictions about the sanctity of marriage and the purity of the believer are formed in the conscience. Those convictions, then, are manifested in the conduct—and true love waits!

Once again, please understand that I'm not championing here for shepherds to neglect the responsibility of offering practical instruction for daily living. Such would be a denial of part of the nature of preaching. I'm simply saying that such application is not the goal of preaching but the natural result of it. Consequently, it must be a servant to the proclamation of biblical truth that feeds the character and alters the conscience. Life change doesn't take place as a result of practical application. Life change takes place as individuals are transformed by biblical truth and then it is manifested in practical application.

No preacher will ever be able to scratch the surface of the infinite amount of variables in the application of God's truth. We could deliver sermons from now until Christ's coming that are filled with how-to instructions and action-driven tasks, and we would never be able to exhaust the host of life situations that our people will encounter during their days on earth. No preacher is that smart. Again, that's at least one of the reasons Jesus gave us His Spirit when He checked out of here bodily. He knew that if He gave believers His presence— the very source of His wisdom and grace—then they would have a constant resource for acting in keeping with His character and will.

Preaching for Christ's Community

The fourth and final manifestation of incarnational preaching may be the most neglected because it's the most difficult to measure. I'm speaking of forming Christ in the community of faith itself, not just the individual believers. When you go to Wal-Mart, a shopping mall, a popular restaurant, or a sporting event in a large arena, you find yourself in the midst of a lot of activity. You're likely to see elaborate facilities and the latest technology. Large numbers of people will be gathered together either enjoying themselves with entertainment or, at the very least, checking things off of their "to do" lists. And whether it's with a favorite product, food, or football team, they'll all be getting their needs met and their desires satisfied.

I can assure you, however, that there's one thing that won't be happening at those places—community. Oh, there may be pockets of isolated community being developed among groups of family members or friends, but the entire group of people gathered at any of those places won't even be thinking about it. It's the same way in the church—we actually can reach lots of people, gather large crowds, build big buildings, develop cutting-edge programs, and even meet the needs of individuals without ever even thinking about developing a corporate consciousness or a sense of common bond within the congregation. Most people aren't interested in being shaped into a corporate body, nor are they concerned with corporate values or goals. That's why contemporary preaching desperately needs a larger purpose than mere individual assent and personal application.

The loss of community is one of the most overlooked realities of contemporary church growth. Consequently, there is a great need for shepherds to give serious attention to forming Christ in the congregation through preaching. When the apostle Paul confessed, "I labor in birth again until Christ is formed in you" (Gal. 4:19), he used his customary plural form of the second-person pronoun ("you"). He intentionally sought to build communities as opposed to merely forming private morality. When he was not reflecting on any particular crisis in the church, Paul was addressing the fundamental questions that had always been at the forefront of Israel's consciousness—*Who are we and what are we to do?*[9] And those are still significant questions for Christian communities today. And surely the answers are loftier than just having a happy home, developing good working relationships, experiencing financial freedom, and so forth.

Today, it seems that the relevant thing to do is make the listening audience—whether seeker or finder—to believe that we are all on the same page. We want everyone to know that we have the same problems, we speak the same language, and we're all on the same journey. We don't want anyone who visits our church to feel any different than our members. But in our sincere efforts we fail to realize that it works the opposite way as well. We unknowingly communicate to members that they're no different than the pagans who come in from the outside. But they are different. They are a covenant community that is the very house of God and the true bride of Christ!

One blatant example of the contrast between preaching for Christ's community and some contemporary preaching can be seen in sermon terminology. Today we are told, "Don't use terminology that is unfamiliar to people who might not have grown up in church," and, "Communicate in the language of the culture." The natural result has been the loss of many terms—and their distinctive meanings—that serve to define the community of faith and set it apart from the surrounding culture. The growing biblical illiteracy of our society has convinced us that we must translate all of our terminology for the benefit of those who do not know our theological lingo. It is highly unlikely that corporate identity will ever be developed without nurturing the community's own distinctive vocabulary.

Without a doubt, the apostle Paul was equipped with the best education available. Consequently, he was more than capable of using the language of his culture and even translating the church's vocabulary into the language of the day. But that didn't keep him from educating his listeners in their own lingo because he knew that owning their own terminology was a necessary characteristic of communities that were bonded together. So he intentionally used and explained terms like "election" (1 Thess. 1:4; 1 Cor. 9–11) and "sanctification" (1 Thess. 3:13; 4:3, 7; 5:23; 1 Cor. 5:1–11:1).[10]

Another danger zone in Christian congregational life is the demise of communal living among believers. Oh, I'm not speaking of the Christian communism which some have mistakenly drawn from the Acts 2:42–47 passage. Such was not the order of the day, even for the early church. What I am championing for, however, is at least some semblance of accepted community standards among God's people and preaching that seeks to establish them.

One of the toughest things that my wife and I deal with as parents is the apparent loss of community among the people of faith in our Christian circles. And we know that we're part of the problem. For example, if we establish a family rule that we don't watch movies above a particular rating, our children don't have to go very far in our community to find a respected Christian family whose children are allowed to see movies with higher (or lower!) ratings. Or if we establish a particular curfew, our kids inevitably have good Christian friends whose parents let them stay out later or require them to be in earlier. And you can guess the response we are sure to get when we attempt to explain our ethical, spiritual, or even biblical rationale for certain rules: "Well, so-and-so's parents let them do it, and they're good Christians!" I don't have much of a problem explaining to my kids the differing standards between the world and the church. But the wide range of ethical norms within the community of faith presents some interesting dilemmas for Christian parents.

While I am in no way suggesting here that local congregations should require adherence to some standardized, legalistic code of conduct for membership, I do want to suggest that moral norms are one of the ways we identify communities and establish boundaries for them. Consequently, pastoral preaching somehow has to move beyond individual instruction and announce ethical mandates that describe morality in communal terms. The congregational shepherd must lead his flock to ask "What should *we* do?" instead of

"What should *I* do?"[11] Shepherds must preach in such a way as to do their part in establishing such a code as determined by careful exegesis of both Scripture and culture.

One final aspect of preaching to shape congregations cannot be overlooked. It's the "big picture" of community existence among believers. The teaching shepherd must preach on a larger plane than merely meeting individual needs and answering individual questions. While there will always be a plethora of topics from which to choose in this realm, the pastor has a loftier goal in his preaching—his congregation's ultimate welfare at Christ's coming. Christ's community must continually be looking for His return.

Many contemporary preachers and listeners have cast stones at the simple faith expressed in some of the great gospel hymns like "When We All Get to Heaven" and "On Jordan's Stormy Banks." But such were the songs that were born in a Christian generation that at least understood that this world was not their home. The church of Jesus Christ has always understood that it was just passing through. Every time the teaching shepherd steps into the pulpit, he must climb to the top of the mountain, cast a wishful eye on the heavenly promised land, and beckon his weary listeners to keep looking expectantly for Christ's return. And those of us who listen to sermons must be ready to follow. That kind of vision shapes individual believers into faith congregations!

Where Do I Go from Here . . .

Now that you have completed the journey through the biblical foundation for pastoral preaching and the philosophy of shepherding, you may proceed in one of two ways as indicated by the shaded areas on the chart below. If you desire to continue with the thematic development of the book, proceed to the introduction to part 3, "Passion-Driven Sermonology," and then to chapter 7, "Preaching as Worship." The (➡) symbol indicates the development of the *goal* in preaching from the practical standpoint. If you choose this path, proceed to chapter 9, "Preaching for Eternity." Once again, be sure to read the introduction to part 3, "Passion-Driven Sermonology," if you have not previously done so along this route.

Table 6.1

	PART 1 (Biblical)		PART 2 (Philosophical)		PART 3 (Practical)
(Content)	Chapter 1: The Message of Preaching ▼	➡	Chapter 4: The Shepherd's Stewardship ▼	➡	Chapter 7: Preaching as Worship ▼
(Resource)	Chapter 2: The Means for Preaching ▼	➡	Chapter 5: The Shepherd's Power ▼	➡	Chapter 8: Preaching with Potency ▼
(Goal)	Chapter 3: The Motive in Preaching	➡	Chapter 6: The Shepherd's Relevance	➡	Chapter 9: Preaching for Eternity

Part 3

PASSION-DRIVEN SERMONOLOGY

"Thus saith the Lord!" This phrase has been the battle cry of preachers since preaching's inauguration in Hebrew prophecy. We have used it to describe what we do—speak for God. Not only have we used it to describe our work in preaching, but those who listen to our sermons have grown to view what we do through this lens. In other words, when the preacher stands to preach, by and large the people in the pew perceive him to be speaking the words of God. What an incredible responsibility! Consequently, preaching for the glory of God calls the shepherd to say only what God said.

The shepherd's understanding of this role has direct bearing on how he approaches sermon development and presentation. If we assume the freedom and responsibility to reveal new, extrabiblical information as demanded by the wants and needs of listeners, and we are completely dependent upon our own ability to affect people's lives, then anything and everything goes with regard to homiletical form and delivery style. On the other hand, if we have been entrusted with an objective body of information—*God's stuff*—our responsibility is simply to communicate that information in a way that is as close to the way it was revealed as possible.

One of the misconceptions many pastors have is that they have been called to prepare and deliver sermons. Because the sermon has become the icon of preaching, numerous pastors have fallen into the trap of equating the two. They make statements like "I've got to get a sermon ready for Sunday" or "I'm working on my sermon for this week" or "I'm preparing a new sermon series." Sermons have come to be equated with preaching, and consequently some pastors often spend more of their time and energy learning to be sermon-meisters than they do learning to be preachers.

Actually, God did not call the pastor to prepare and deliver sermons; He called him to preach! And those two activities are not necessarily the same thing. A sermon is technically just a public discourse, usually of a religious nature. It can be about anything, Christian or non-Christian, moral or immoral, ethical or unethical. Preaching can only be about the Word. Sermons can be preserved in books. Preaching can't. Anybody can prepare and deliver a sermon. It is true that everyone who truly preaches delivers sermons. But not everyone who prepares and delivers sermons actually preaches.

Authentic preaching and the sermons that carry it really have to be defined by the right *message*, the right *means*, and the right *motive*. Authentic preaching is passion-driven preaching. Maybe such preaching could be defined as a God-called man with a God-given message, driven by a God-glorifying passion, empowered by a God-endowed Spirit, aimed at a God-given faith. Only men whose messages are rooted in those realities are truly preaching! Then and only then should *sermons* and *preaching* be a part of the same conversation.

When a passion-driven shepherd prepares and delivers sermons, his messages take on a whole new nature. He is not merely delivering his own public discourse; he is serving as a mouthpiece for the public discourse of the Almighty. As both pastor and people understand this stewardship that has been given to them and rely on its supernatural nature, then sermons contain the highest of relevance. Such an understanding adds a bit of a different meaning to the sermon, and it elevates our motivation for studying it to an entirely different plane.

The biblical foundation and philosophical framework of the preaching event ultimately will determine the very nature of the pastor's sermons, as well as how the listeners receive them. So, now we are ready to let our scripturology and our shepherdology determine our *sermonology*. As sermons become a sacrifice of praise in worship to the glory of God, then pastors can preach with spiritual power for an eternal cause. And transformed listeners will find themselves as living manifestations of the glory of God!

CHAPTER 7

Preaching as Worship:
BIBLICAL EXPOSITION

Modern evangelical Christianity owes much to the younger generations who have fostered the revival of corporate worship we've experienced over the past few decades. The lifeless expressions of worship that characterized many churches were sad commentaries on some Christians' perspectives of God. It has been invigorating to see the increase in congregational participation, the variation in musical expression, and the focus on ministering to the Lord instead of just one another. Being the people of extremes we are, however, the danger exists that we will allow the pendulum to swing too far. Quite often in corporate worship services I see many Christians coming really close to worshiping "worship." Just think about some of the manifestations of this perversion—referring only to musical praise as "worship," designating only musicians as "worship leaders," and drawing an obvious distinction between "worship" and "preaching" in corporate services.

While all of these seem harmless, they have contributed greatly to a de-emphasis on preaching as an expression of worship. One only has to observe some worshipers standing with raised hands and closed eyes during a segment of musical praise, only to sit restlessly with no Bible in hand during the sermon. What could possibly bring more honor to God than for His people to hear and revere His voice? I submit that the teaching shepherd is the primary worship leader in the congregation, and the sermon is a significant sacrifice of praise offered by both the pastor in the pulpit and the people in the pew. Although I use the terms "pulpit" and "pew" metaphorically, they represent the reality of magnifying God's voice in Christian worship!

Magnifying God's Voice in the Pulpit

I have realized something about my own ministry in recent years that has vaulted me on a journey to reform my preaching. I embarrassingly became aware that my walk with Christ had digressed to the point of studying the Bible only because I was responsible for preparing and delivering a sermon. But when I look at the lives and ministries of the reformers—the Luthers and Calvins and Zwinglis—I realize that they prepared and delivered sermons because they studied the Bible. To say it another way, I often study the Bible because I've got to preach. The reformers preached because they were immersed in the Bible. They *had* to preach because they were consumed and compelled by the Scriptures! I want to preach like the reformers.

For that to happen, I will need to be caught up once again in God's Word and His calling upon my life to preach it. When that happens, the art of sermonizing will take its rightful place as the natural outgrowth of my journey. I will not be getting the cart before the horse, thinking too much about sermon-making and presentation and too little about discerning God's voice. Consequently, the sermon as worship begins in the pastor's study as a personal encounter with God! Then, it is offered as a sacrifice of praise when it is delivered to the congregation. Let me offer two foundational moorings for this two-fold experience.

Maximize What God Is Saying

V. L. Stanfield, one of my great forefathers in preaching at New Orleans Baptist Theological Seminary, described preaching as "giving the Bible a voice."[1] The sermon as worship begins for the pastor in discovering the voice of God. He must ask the question, *"What is God saying?"* When the eternal truth of God is revealed, the people in essence are hearing the very voice of God instead of the voice of the preacher. Regarding the preaching and teaching gifts, Peter said, "If anyone speaks, let him speak as the oracles of God" (1 Pet. 4:11).

If preaching is the act of giving the Bible a voice, then the Bible could be described as giving God a voice. So if the Bible is God's voice, and preaching is the Bible's voice, then the sermon by necessity and integrity must reflect the very voice of God. H. C. Brown Jr. said that the basic question to be asked about a sermon is: "'Who said it?' That is, does the preacher speak from the Bible or merely from his own experience? . . . Therefore, one must always ask about a sermon, 'Who said it? The preacher or the Bible?'"[2]

But how does one hear the voice of God in the Bible, and ultimately how is that voice maximized in the sermon? The answer to that question drives us straight to the default approach to pastoral preaching—the exposition of biblical texts. God's voice has to be exposed if He is to be magnified, and the bread and butter of the pastor's weekly menu must be given to that end. By exposition I am referring to the process of laying open a biblical text in such a way that its original meaning—*God's voice*—is brought to bear on the lives of contemporary listeners. The word *expose* means "to lay open or uncover," and it implies the sum of the preacher's exegesis, hermeneutics, and homiletics.

When I was in junior high school, we studied fossils. One of the things I discovered about fossils is that they often are preserved for thousands and thousands of years by being protected within the layers of sediment between which they were sandwiched. The discovery of the fossils comes about by the process of digging through the sedimentary layers. In other words, paleontologists and archeologists dig through the layers until the fossil is exposed. But one of the coolest things I remember about that whole study was being shown some pictures and models of those fossils embedded within several layers. Sometimes we saw pictures or models with a view from above, showing a fossil or an impression embedded within layers of sediment. Sometimes we saw pictures or models that showed a cross section of the layers. That whole process greatly enhanced my understanding of the fossil itself and the role that it played in history.

God's revelation was given thousands and thousands of years ago. In addition to a radically different time period than our own, His Word was revealed in a vast array of languages, cultures, settings, backgrounds, worldviews, and a host of other contextual factors. Since that time, this revelation has been covered up with layer upon layer of even more of the same kinds of factors. Each generation in each part of the world has approached the Word of God with its own combination of language, cultural norms, social setting, as well as both political and religious worldviews. When you stop and think about it, the variables are almost infinite. And all of that has covered over the truth and relevance of God's Word revealed long ago.

When people look at the Bible today, often times all they see is the layers. And their logical conclusion is, "The Bible is irrelevant!" The pastor's role is to be the paleontologist and archeologist who digs through the layers to get at the truth. He peels back the layers of language, culture, background, worldview, and more, in order to expose the truth and all its relevance for today. This makes exposition more than a sermon form defined by the length of a given text, a particular rhetorical form, or a Bible book series. Exposition is a journey that begins long before the sermon is developed or preached. Essentially, exposition describes the manner of treatment with which Scripture is handled, a process by which the pastor discovers and encounters the true voice of God. When the preacher embarks upon this journey with integrity, he essentially hears the voice of God through the mind of the Holy Spirit in the given biblical text.

In the sermon that is birthed from this process, the pastor shows enough of his journey to his listeners—sometimes from above, sometimes from the side—to enhance their understanding of the truth and the role it plays in their lives. Regarding the desperate need for these kinds of sermons in the twenty-first-century church, Joseph Stowell observed:

> It should concern us that increasingly, preaching in America today is being postured as more of a self-help values lecture with periodic tips of the hat to Scripture references than it is to a clear exposition of the truth of the authoritative Word of God. . . . When the church gathers as the body of Christ, it needs to be taught the Word of God. For in that is the only real power of transformational growth and development to the glory of Christ.[3]

As the pastor takes his people on a journey into God's Word, he magnifies God's voice, brings glory to Him, and exposes his listeners to supernatural truth that can change their lives.

One of the incredible privileges I have as dean of the chapel at our school is to be able to preach in chapel just about every week. In addition to pastoring a local church nearby, I get to be somewhat of a teaching pastor to our seminary family. While the joy is beyond description, I must admit that it can be a bit intimidating preaching regularly to both ministerial students and faculty members, many of whom are ministers themselves. After listening to me preach each week for the better part of a year, one of my colleagues baffled me with a question one afternoon as we were leaving the office. He said, "Where did you get your convictions about biblical preaching?" No one had ever asked me that question in my twenty years as a preacher. Not wanting to appear to have never thought through such a basic issue for a preaching professor, I quickly identified some of the great preachers who had influenced me over the years.

But throughout the evening I could not get the question out of my mind, and I finally admitted to myself that I had responded too quickly and incompletely. My father was not a preacher. The pastors under which I sat during my formative years would not have been considered expositors in the truest sense of the term. I did not respond to God's call to preach until I was in college, but it really was not even until much later that I began to pay any attention to the differences in style between preachers. After several hours of my somewhat nostalgic mental journey, I finally landed on the real answer to my friend's question. The next day I pulled him aside and told him my matured conclusion: My parents raised me to believe that the Bible is God's inerrant, infallible, and inspired Word. When I started preaching, the thing that seemed to make the most sense to me was to do it in such a way that my words were as close as possible to the Words that God had said. That is what our sermons should be—as close as possible to the Words that God said! So pastors must maximize the voice of God in their sermons.

Minimize What God Is Not Saying

Equally important for the sermon, as worship, is to limit attention to what God is *not* saying in the biblical text. If the sermon is to be offered as a sacrifice of praise to the Father, we must be sure that it does not magnify things that God did not say. The prevention of such a travesty also begins in the pastor's encounter with the biblical text in his study long before the sermon is preached. There he will not only determine to maximize what God is saying but to minimize attention to what God is not saying.

What the pastor believes about the essence and agenda of the Bible will have direct bearing on the way he approaches it in his study and the purpose for which he uses it in his sermons. For example, if he believes the Bible is a practical manual for daily living, then he will study it as such. And most of his sermons will fall out as how-to addresses on the plethora of the day to day struggles of humanity. If the pastor believes the Bible is strictly for the purpose of bringing people to salvation, then his sermon repertoire is likely to be weighted heavily with evangelistic messages. And on and on we could go. On the other hand, if the pastor believes God's agenda in the Bible is the re-creation of humanity, then he is free simply to let it speak in keeping with that end so that it might do its supernatural work in the lives of those who hear.

A great example of this distinction can be seen in the subject of Christian *leadership* today. When that topic is raised, most of our minds immediately gravitate toward the Book of Nehemiah. Yes, Nehemiah and leadership are almost synonymous. As pastors and other church leaders scramble to fill the undeniable leadership void in congregations everywhere, this Bible book is frequently preached and taught as a resource manual for developing leaders. After all, the Book of Nehemiah is God's textbook on the subject. Or is it?

A careful consideration of Nehemiah certainly reveals some principles that can be applied to the development of leaders in the kingdom and elsewhere. Yet exegetical integrity refuses to allow us to conclude that the provision of leadership principles is the reason this book found its way into the Canon of inspired Scripture. A closer look will reveal that this book is about how God sovereignly works to preserve the community of faith, and how He uses a willing servant along the way to experience His faithfulness in accomplishing the task (cf. Neh. 1:10; 2:8, 18; 4:15; 7:5). First and foremost, this book is about Him, not us!

Furthermore, our obsession with the practical can get us into serious trouble with interpretation and application. The hermeneutical slight of hand necessary to feature the practical implications of Scripture often runs into major inconsistency. Consider Nehemiah's approach to leadership toward the end of the book: "I contended with them and cursed them, struck some of them and pulled out their hair, and made them swear by God" (Neh. 13:25). Try applying that approach to leadership in your next church business meeting! Reality is, however, that such a leadership approach would be conveniently overlooked in most sermons on the subject.

Such a treatment of the biblical text is nothing more than careless hermeneutical gymnastics. Tragically, it often results in discouragement, frustration, and even anger at God on the part of some listeners when the pastor's human wisdom does not hold up in certain situations. Worse yet, people who listen to such treatment of the Bible week after week receive no *God stuff*—no voice from the mountain to effect supernatural life change—but instead a mere smorgasbord of *good stuff* that fattens the natural man without nourishing the soul.

Pastors must realize, and be OK with the fact that God never intended Scripture to address every issue in life or to answer every question that man may raise. Common sense alone tells us that the Bible was never meant to answer all the questions people are asking nor to resource them with specific direction for every circumstance that might be encountered in life. Even the apostle John, under the inspiration of the Holy Spirit, admitted that it would have been impossible to record in many volumes all of the things that Jesus did during His relatively short life on earth (see John 21:25). Why should we think that practical guidance for the multiplied life experiences of billions of people in generation after generation could be contained in a single volume?

Have you ever thought about the many subjects on which the voice of God in Scripture is silent or the numerous questions the Bible fails to answer? Take dinosaurs, for example. We have fairly good scientific evidence that some time long ago those big creatures roamed the earth. Yet the Bible is mute on the subject. Even if we identify a verse here and there that may entertain the existence of the animals, we are not given any kind of treatment regarding their nature or any conclusive information on their extinction. To be sure, there are plenty of people today who have questions about such matters. The bottom line, however, is that God in His infinite wisdom chose not to talk on that subject in His Word—largely because that is not part of His agenda!

But dinosaurs are not our problem. The issues that haunt us in ministry are closer to home. They are both more *real* and more *relevant* to the people who come to hear us preach. I am speaking about matters like raising kids, building marriages, restoring relationships, managing finances, developing leadership skills, and the like. These are the real-life issues with which our people struggle and about which they serve up many questions. And because we are ministers of the gospel we want to help. We want to resource them with answers to their questions and practical help for groping with their problems. And yet the pastor who desires to speak with any divine authority at all must ask the same fundamental question about these topics and any others about which he ventures to preach: *Does God talk on this subject in His Word?*

In order to minimize what God is not saying, the answers to this question must be determined by more than mere generalizations or secondary applications in the Bible. This approach to Scripture is all too common today. About the crisis in the modern pulpit, Kaiser observed that "many pastors can preach whole messages with little more than a tip of the hat to a clause or two taken from a biblical context that few, if any, recognize."[4] The pastor must be brutally honest about whether or not God speaks on a subject with the same authority with which he plans to communicate it in his sermon. Otherwise the pastor presents the Bible to his flock as merely a collection of principles, any of which can be impressed upon any and every given life situation.

To be sure, contemporary pastors are preaching "out of season." Many pastors are not getting much help from their congregations when it comes to being faithful to this task of simply exposing what God says in the Bible as opposed to subjects remotely associated with the Bible. MacArthur lamented:

> Many congregations, however, do not *want* their pastors to
> preach only the Word. They "will not endure sound doctrine;
> but wanting to have their ears tickled, they will accumulate for
> themselves teachers in accordance to their own desires." . . . As
> one commentator has observed, "In periods of unsettled faith,

skepticism, and mere curious speculation in matters of religion, teachers of all kinds swarm like the flies in Egypt. The demand creates the supply. The hearers invite and shape their own preachers. If the people desire a calf to worship, a ministerial calf-maker is readily found." Some people, including some immature believers, will go from church to church looking for the right preacher. Unfortunately their idea of "right" preaching is not sound biblical exposition but interesting observations and suggestions based on the preacher's personal philosophy. They are not looking for a word from God to believe but for a word from man to consider.[5]

People should not come to church to hear sermons that voice the pastor's opinions about politics, psychology, economics, or even religion, including the politics of denominationalism, the psychology of child-rearing and stress management, the economics of financial planning, and the ecumenical religious agenda. They should instead come to hear sermons that expose the voice of God as revealed in the Bible.

Sometimes the voice of God is as clear in the Bible in the things it *does not* say as it is in the things it *does* say. The Bible's silence easily can be replaced, however, with the voices of human wisdom that can be heard just about everywhere. And while there is much good and helpful information in some of those voices that can be used for illustrative and applicatory purposes in the sermon, the pastor must never confuse them with the voice of God or allow them to displace His voice in preaching. It is imperative that pastors minimize their attention to what God is not saying.

Magnifying God's Voice in the Pew

I never will forget the first time I ever went into a Waffle House restaurant and ordered hash brown potatoes. The waitress asked me, "Do you want them scattered, covered, smothered, topped, chunked, or diced?" I never knew there were that many ways to fix hash browns! Had I read the menu carefully I would have noticed the important distinctions between the various forms. "Scattered" simply refers to their position on the plate. "Covered" and "smothered" means they are served with cheese or onions respectively. "Topped" means they are covered with chili. "Chunked" means they are mixed with ham, and "diced" means they are mixed with tomatoes. While pastors are not in the business of preparing Idaho's best, we do need to know the difference between preaching when the church is *gathered* and preaching when the church is *scattered*. The New Testament seems to make a distinction between the two.

The church *gathers* at regular and organized times as believers withdraw from the world for edification and worship. The church *scatters* as believers merge back into the world of work, school, and play, becoming again part of a medley of regenerate and unregenerate people. While the focus when the church is *scattered* should ever be on the salvation of sinners, we have a unique opportunity to experience God when the church is *gathered* for its corporate worship services. As the pastor faithfully magnifies God's voice in the expository sermon, God's Spirit partners with His Word to draw people to Himself. In His presence, the Word should inspire listeners to praise, awe, and conviction.

Revere the Word with Praise

Several years ago I preached a sermon in which I used a Nike tennis shoe as an object lesson for the Greek verb translated *conquered* or *prevailed* (*nikano*; see Rev. 5:5). At one point during the message I set the tennis shoe down next to my Bible. After the service, a young Christian woman who had immigrated here from the Middle East spoke to me.

She complimented me on the sermon but then proceeded to tell me that she was offended when I set the tennis shoe on the same surface as the Bible. She went on to explain that in her country no Christian would dare set something as holy as God's Word on the same surface with dusty feet. She also commented on how appalled she was to observe in our American worship services how adults placed their Bibles on the floor for convenience and students slung them across pews to save seats. While I knew that one could carry such accusations too far, I must admit that I was quite humbled.

Someone once said that familiarity breeds contempt. I often wonder if the convenience, availability, and easy accessibility of the Bible in free regions of the world like the United States have not caused some of us to stoop to new levels of irreverence for it. Worse yet, I wonder if our apparent irreverence of the physical book says anything about the value we place on its contents or the praise we offer to it. Worst of all, I wonder if the lack of *God's stuff* in many sermons today has caused the presence of both of these factors to diminish in contemporary worship. These two responses—*reverence* and *praise*—are both due God's Word and should naturally follow when His voice is magnified through exposition.

During Israel's return from exile and subsequent revival of worship in the community of faith, Ezra and Nehemiah nurtured in God's people a *reverence* for the Book of God. At one point "all the people gathered together as one man in the open square that was in front of the Water Gate; and they told Ezra the scribe to bring the Book of the Law of Moses, which the LORD had commanded Israel" (Neh. 8:1). The way these people longed for the Scriptures is astounding, and they exemplified a reverence for them that so desperately needs to be recovered in our day. Consider how those of us who listen to preaching should respond when God's voice is magnified in the sermon.

First, we must view the Scriptures as God's Word, not man's. Notice that they requested "the Book of the Law of Moses, which the LORD had commanded" (Neh. 8:1). The people equated Moses' words with God's Words! When the Bible is preached as God's Word and His voice is magnified, we must receive it as such instead of just the words of man. But if the sermons you hear are just filled with *good stuff,* you will easily grow accustomed to hearing the thoughts, opinions, and ideas of the preacher or his sources. Those kinds of sermons veil the voice of God. While we don't have to agree on every single point of interpretation, as the people of God we better agree on inspiration if we want to hear His voice in sermons.

Second, we must allow the Scriptures to unite us, not divide us. Of all the things that could have divided these people, of all the variety of opinions they certainly possessed, they gathered to hear God's Law "as one man" (Neh. 8:1). That says something about their view of and reverence for God's Word. When it came to what God said, there was no argument, only unity. That didn't mean everything was immediately clear or that there was no room for discussion. The rest of this passage makes that plain. It did mean, however, that the Scriptures were a rallying point for them. They were the hub around which their very beings revolved. Don't allow lesser issues to create factions between you and other believers who embrace the Bible as God's inerrant, infallible Word!

Third, we must make the Scriptures our choice, not a chore. Now I'm not saying that we ought never to require our children or even others to read or listen to the Bible on certain occasions. But it seems that for many of us it's a burden to spend personal time in God's Word, to bring our Bibles to church, or to sit through a sermon. Notice who requested the sermon. Not Ezra or Nehemiah; not one of the scribes or Levites. The people did! "They told Ezra . . . to bring the Book" (Neh. 8:1). That should be our heart cry when we go to a worship service: "Bring the Book!" And many preachers are bringing everything but the Book in their sermons. Listen, friend, there's a void in every one of us that can only be filled by the divine, and it cries out for a Word from Him. We ought to be hungry to hear a Word from God, to know what the Bible says. Let your pastor know that you're not interested in coming to church to hear *good stuff*. Tell him to bring you *God's stuff!*

Not only did Ezra and Nehemiah foster a reverence for God's Word, their faithfulness in bringing it to the people inspired praise of the Scriptures from them. The sermon event recorded in Nehemiah 8 prompted a phenomenal response on the part of the listeners that really shows how much they valued God's Word. When Ezra prayed and prepared to read the Scriptures, "all the people stood up. . . . All the people answered, 'Amen, Amen!' while lifting up their hands. . . . They bowed their heads and worshiped the LORD with their faces to the ground" (Neh. 8:5–6). When was the last time you or people around you responded that way when the pastor got up to preach a sermon?

But here is what's most interesting. Did you notice that these responses are all ones that we normally associate with musical worship? Yet they weren't offered in response to music but in anticipation of hearing a word from the Lord! I'm well aware that preachers have been guilty for years of minimizing, and even downplaying, the role of musical worship for the sake of magnifying the preaching event. But it appears that the pendulum may have swung in our day, even to the point of restricting our understanding of "worship" to the musical presence in our services. In this text, it's clearly not music but the Word that inspires, expresses, and defines worship.

One of the reasons for this response of praise is because the Bible makes little distinction between God and His Word when it comes to the praise offered by His people. In recent years, some Christians have become concerned that the renewed emphasis on biblical authority would lead to bibliolatry, or the worship of the Bible. But based upon His Word, God probably isn't nearly as concerned about that possibility as we have become. The psalmist said:

> In God (I will praise His word),
> In God I have put my trust (Ps. 56:4);

and

> In God (I will praise His word),
> In the LORD (I will praise His word) (Ps. 56:10);

and

> My hands also I will lift up to Your commandments,
> Which I love,
> And I will meditate on Your statutes (Ps. 119:48);

and

> My flesh trembles for fear of You,
> And I am afraid of Your judgments (Ps. 119:120),

and maybe most astounding of all,

> I will worship toward Your holy temple,
> And praise Your name
> For Your lovingkindness and Your truth;
> For You have magnified Your word above all Your name
> (Ps. 138:2).

These are just a few of the many examples of how Scripture makes little distinction between God and His Word (see also Ps. 119:9–11, 49–50, 97–98, 123, 137–144; 130:5–6). When we praise His Word, we are praising Him. So when His voice is magnified in the sermon, God draws people to Himself. Oh, how we need to reclaim the role of Scripture reading and expository preaching in corporate worship, and how we need to revere God's Word with praise when it is proclaimed!

Fear the Word with Awe

When we begin to develop a desperate need to hear the voice of God in worship, He has a tendency to show up. And when He shows up, it does something to us. The early chapters of Acts describe certain events which took place shortly after the church's birth at Pentecost. These events appear to indicate that the voice of God as spoken by the apostles in the midst of God's people caused believers and unbelievers alike to stand in fear and awe of God's presence. As God's voice is magnified through biblical exposition, those of us who listen to such preaching are likely to find ourselves responding in similar fashion.

While we must always be careful not to view the infant church birthed in Acts 2 as the complete model of what the church was intended to be, it is important to note the natural response to its new life. After all, there we see the germinal church in its purest form, before it had the opportunity to be tainted by humanity (e.g., see Acts 5:1–11 and 6:1). After the great evangelistic harvest recorded in Acts 2:41, Luke notes in the next verse that the new converts "continued steadfastly in the apostles' doctrine and fellowship, in the breaking of bread, and in prayers." The structure of the paragraph introduced by this statement indicates that these four activities were the nonnegotiable activities of the earliest Christian congregation.

The apostles made much of schooling the people in the teachings of Christ and their implications for godly living, the doctrine which became the foundation on which the church was built (see Acts 6:2–4; Eph. 2:20). The new community practiced authentic fellowship—biblical *koinonia*—as they took radical measures to care for one another's needs (see Acts 2:44–45; 4:32–37). They celebrated their hope in Christ's atoning death and His imminent return through communion (see Matt. 26:26–29; 1 Cor. 11:23–26), a ceremony which certainly was the germination of the church's corporate worship life. And they expressed their utter dependence upon their Lord through seemingly incessant prayer (see John 14:12–14 and Acts 1:14, 24; 3:1).

Interestingly, there is a stark contrast in this passage regarding the trend in our day to design the church's regular meetings for seekers. All four of these nonnegotiable activities actually were activities for believers. Through them, believers were edified and spiritually nourished to go out and proclaim the gospel to unbelievers. There is no indication that the focus of any of these activities was for the expressed purpose of evangelism. There is not even any indication that they were consumed with musical preferences like we are, much less allowing them to be driven by the current culture! While they most likely utilized music as part of their worship, they apparently were not overly concerned with whether or not their musical style was germane to outsiders. And as we have already determined, the evangelism that resulted appears to be that which the Lord brought about as a result of their devotion to these four activities.

The subsequent verses go on to "flesh out" the first two priorities of the church in its infancy, namely the apostles' doctrine (see Acts 2:43) and fellowship (see Acts 2:44–47). For our purposes, it is especially important to note that the first thing mentioned on the list is the apostles' doctrine. This no doubt is a reference to the divine revelation that they taught, comprised of their inspired reflection on the life and ministry of the Lord Jesus Christ and subsequent interpretation of the Old Testament Scriptures. Later in Ephesians, Paul placed the teaching of these apostles alongside that of the New Testament prophets and called it the very foundation on which the church is built (see Eph. 2:20). The unique function of these human instruments was to authoritatively speak the word of God to the church in the years before the New Testament Canon was complete. Its written form no doubt is the New Testament we have today.

The people's response to these germinal Christian worship services was one of "fear" (Acts 2:43). The word describes the awe or holy terror that resulted from their sense of divine presence. It includes the attitude of reverence that is birthed when people realize deity is present (cf. Luke 7:16; Acts 5:5,11; Luke 7:16). These gatherings of the early Christians were so authentic and spiritually infused that apparently believers and unbelievers were in awe. And they were not awed by buildings, budgets, music, programs, or anything like that, but by the supernatural presence of God.

The primary manifestation that prompted the awe obviously was the "many wonders and signs [which] were done through the apostles" (Acts 2:43). It is vitally important for us to understand the relationship between these miracles and the preaching of the Word. These apostolic miracles primarily served two purposes. First, they attracted attention and pointed to spiritual truth, especially the deity of Jesus (cf. John 14:10–12; Acts 9:32–35, 42). Second, God attended the preaching of Jesus, the apostles, and some of their close associates with miracles to confirm that they were indeed speaking for Him (cf. Acts 2:22; Heb. 2:3–4; 2 Cor. 12:12).

The exposition of God's voice in written Scripture serves the same purposes today. The Bible points to spiritual truth and testifies of Jesus' divinity. And today the Bible determines who is speaking with the voice of God as we compare the sermons of contemporary preachers with the text of Holy Scripture! As sermons are delivered that are consistent with the intended meaning of the text of the Bible, God's voice is magnified. Whenever that happens, those of us who hear ought to be in awe. When that happens, the sermon becomes worship!

Another event that has implications for our worshipful response to God's Word is the judgment of Ananias and Sapphira recorded in Acts 5:1–11. The ramifications of that occurrence are recorded in the subsequent verses. Luke recorded that "through the hands of the apostles many signs and wonders were done among the people. And they were all with one accord in Solomon's Porch. Yet none of the rest dared join them, but the people esteemed them highly. And believers were increasingly added to the Lord, multitudes of both men and women" (Acts 5:12–14). Once again, careful study of Acts and the rest of the New Testament reveals that the "signs and wonders" were primarily God's confirmation of the preached Word.

Here we see the same fear and awe in response to the voice of God as it was proclaimed. As with the new church after Pentecost, unbelievers were welcome at these church gatherings, but only from the standpoint of observation and investigation. The people kept their distance with healthy respect. The people were awed by the power of the apostles and the message they preached, so much so that the "seekers" did not hurry to join the Christian band in the colonnade but remained on the perimeter. In other words, most of the unbelievers chose not to make a commitment to the group. The determining factor appeared to be the degree of commitment an individual was willing to make. The crowd respectfully kept its distance until they were ready to submit and *commit* to the gospel's power, for the fate of Ananias and Sapphira showed how perilous vain or halfhearted allegiance might be. Such is another rebuke of contemporary efforts to "dumb down" the church's worship for the sake of unbelievers!

When the church gathered in Acts with a focus on proclaiming God's Word, He showed up in a unique way. As the Word was preached, even unbelievers were drawn by the supernatural power of God. And they stood in awe of His presence. And once again we have absolutely no biblical evidence that the believers focused their attention during these regular corporate gatherings on evangelistic activity. That was their agenda when the church scattered into the marketplace and into the formal Jewish worship events. At those places they spontaneously engaged in evangelistic preaching and dialogue with unbelievers (e.g., Acts 3:1–26; 4:1–22; 6:8–7:60; 8:4–13, 26–40).

For us, the parallel is not to the signs and wonders, but to the validation of God's voice through the exposition of Scripture. A devotion to the apostles' teaching through expository sermons is foundational for accommodating a worshipful response on the part of God's people. God designed the local church to be a place where His voice is exposed. This early church sat under the teaching ministry of the apostles, and consequently, this same doctrine must inform the sermons of all pastors today, and those of us who listen to them should respond in awe of the presence of God.

Dear friend, be encouraged. Your pastor does not have to compromise the preaching of God's Word or authentic worship to supernaturally impact those who are present—including seekers! When God is glorified in the proclamation of the Bible, His Spirit is free to do His supernatural work. Then His presence will be thick in the surroundings. And when God's presence is demonstrated, then those of us who listen to sermons will recognize it and respect it.

Hear the Word with Conviction

As the church matured, the emphasis on magnifying God's voice continued, and yet Christians maintained their sensitivity to the presence of seekers as well. But something else also continued—cultivating an atmosphere during Christian worship services that was thick with the presence of God! If the attendees who frequented the Jerusalem assembly were filled with a sense of holy awe, the ones who attended the Corinthian gatherings approximately two decades later found themselves overwhelmed with deep conviction which often led to repentance.

Paul's first letter to the Corinthians addressed circumstances within the local church that help us to see the same priority being placed on magnifying God's voice during corporate worship. In his comparison of certain spiritual gifts, Paul emphasized the superiority of prophecy over tongues in public worship:

> Therefore tongues are for a sign, not to those who believe but to unbelievers; but prophesying is not for unbelievers but for those who believe. Therefore if the whole church comes together in one place, and all speak with tongues, and there come in those who are uninformed or unbelievers, will they not say that you are out of your mind? But if all prophesy, and an unbeliever or an uninformed person comes in, he is convinced by all, he is convicted by all. And thus the secrets of his heart are revealed; and so, falling down on his face, he will worship God and report that God is truly among you. . . . Let all things be done for edification (1 Cor. 14:22–26).

Once again, the example of the New Testament reveals how pastoral preaching can edify believers and at the same time prompt conviction in everyone in attendance—including seekers!

It is extremely important for us to understand the role conviction plays in both the worship of believers and the salvation of seekers. Obviously, there is a modern infatuation, yea, obsession, in contemporary church growth ideology with using worship as a means of evangelism. One of the tragedies of such an approach is the erroneous rearranging of the crucial phases of the Pauline perspective mentioned in the text.

Regarding Paul's charge to the Corinthians, F. F. Bruce described the response of the unsaved: "On entering a church meeting, he hears all the members speaking words in a language he knows, which pierce direct to his heart and conscience, expose his inmost secrets, and convict him of sin. This, he will say, is God's message for me."[6] In other words, Paul implied that the unbeliever's journey followed this order: attendance, hearing with understanding, conviction, and repentant worship. Today, a subtle reordering of the elements has resulted in the following strategy: attendance, worship, hearing with understanding, and hopefully conviction.

The rearranging of these stages has gone a long way in perverting the content of contemporary pastoral preaching. In Paul's mind, faithful preaching of God's authoritative Word, which determines hearing and understanding, gave birth to conviction, and then conviction gave birth to authentic worship in the context of repentance. In many approaches to contemporary church growth, however, worship defines preaching with the assumption that it will ultimately produce conviction. But as worship is moved up in the process, it ceases to be defined by the theology and doctrine that are communicated only through right preaching. The result is an event instead of an encounter. As an event, worship naturally begins to take on the character of the participants, at least a segment of which are lost. The natural end is that worship becomes culture driven. Everything that follows, then, becomes skewed by the itching ears of the supposed "worshipers," including the preaching and the convicting.

The early Christians knew that genuine worship of God and even recognition of His presence were prefaced by the personal conviction of sin. In Corinth at least, the unbeliever would humble himself, desert his idols or his Jewish religion, and glorify the only true God. This may have happened at once in the meeting of the church or at a later time. Whichever the case, his worship of God was conceived in his conviction of sin.[7] The two activities could not be separated, nor could their order be switched.

Another thing about which the Corinthian assembly reminds us is that preaching is God's primary means of sounding His voice, bringing conviction on listeners, and granting them repentance. Without a doubt, preaching is the most effective means of communicating God's Word to both believers and unbelievers. In fact, this passage implies the superiority of preaching over *all* other means of communicating God's Word to anyone. In the Corinthian context it was to be preferred especially over tongues, a contention that underscores the tremendous worth of good prophetic utterance. The word of the prophet, spoken by the Holy Spirit to believers, demonstrated the presence of God in the services. And that would convict unbelievers and at the very least lead them to acknowledge God's presence, if not genuine repentance! This characteristic alone made preaching superior to other spiritual exercises with regard to relating to believers and unbelievers.

This smacks in the face of many modern efforts to "relate" to worshipers through an overemphasis on other forms of gospel proclamation. While music, drama, "creative movements," and other elements of public worship may play valuable roles in communicating God's voice, working through the preaching of

His Word is God's primary means of bringing people to the conviction that the argument being made is true and that they will be judged on the basis of their response. About this MacArthur noted:

> When the Word is proclaimed it speaks to men's hearts and
> brings conviction of sin, the first step in coming to faith. The
> convicted person comes to see himself as he really is, because
> the secrets of his heart are disclosed. His sinful intentions and
> acts are revealed to him. Consequently, he will fall on his face
> and worship God, declaring that God is certainly among you.
> The church's most powerful testimony is not in its ecstasies, but
> in its clear proclamation of the powerful Word of God.[8]

For the Corinthians, right preaching could not be sacrificed for the sake of other kinds of utterances when it came to communicating to believers or unbelievers.

If the church today is to be biblical in corporate worship, then biblical preaching must be allowed to play the central role in its communication to all who attend. Some have said that the indicator of the church's true success is whether or not God is in the midst of the church. As pastors plainly expose the voice of God in Scripture in language which is intelligible and proper, those of us who listen to sermons will be edified, and the power of God will be demonstrated in the surroundings of worship. To top it all off, we may even begin to find more seekers becoming converted to Christianity!

Christian worship, then, does not have to be adapted to the whims and preferences of the secular heart and mind in order to have evangelistic impact. In fact, the idea that the unregenerate soul should drive the nature of true worship is truly unbiblical indeed. The example of the New Testament church simply suggests that our worship be adapted only to the point of enabling unbelievers to find themselves in the arena of true worship and to hear the voice of God that is being spoken. Such an injunction should drive today's pastors, other worship leaders, and all those who participate in worship to be aggressive and intentional in ensuring that our worship is truly biblical and authentic. That is the only way that anyone—believer or unbeliever—will hear God.

Beloved, we can be confident that the exposition of biblical truth will cultivate spiritual conviction. The clear, persuasive explanation and application of God's Word in the presence of believers and unbelievers in Christian worship services will result in a desirable response on the part of many of those who hear. Certainly, we should do everything we can within the parameters of holiness and appropriateness to persuade lost people to attend our worship services. And when they come, we should make every effort to let them over-hear with understanding the clear voice of God in the Bible. Then and only then can we ensure that God's Spirit and power will be demonstrated, and that the resulting conviction and worship will be real.

Where Do I Go from Here . . .

Now that you have begun to look at the practical aspects of the theology of pas-toral preaching, you may proceed one of two ways as indicated by the shaded areas on the chart below. The (▼) symbol indicates the thematic development of more of these practical implications. If you are following this path, proceed to chapter 8, "Preaching with Potency." If you are following the development of thought from biblical to philosophical to practical, you have finished consider-ation of the *content* of pastoral preaching and can now begin to look at the *resource.* If you are following this path, go back to chapter 2, "The Means for Preaching."

Table 7.1

	PART 1 (Biblical)		PART 2 (Philosophical)		PART 3 (Practical)
(Content)	Chapter 1: The Message of Preaching ▼	➡	Chapter 4: The Shepherd's Stewardship ▼	➡	Chapter 7: Preaching as Worship ▼
(Resource)	Chapter 2: The Means for Preaching ▼	➡	Chapter 5: The Shepherd's Power ▼	➡	Chapter 8: Preaching with Potency ▼
(Goal)	Chapter 3: The Motive in Preaching	➡	Chapter 6: The Shepherd's Relevance	➡	Chapter 9: Preaching for Eternity

CHAPTER 8

Preaching with Potency:

TEXTUAL INTEGRITY

"Somebody please shoot me and let's get this over with!" I can't begin to tell you how many times I have felt that way in the middle of a sermon. Most—actually all—preachers have been there. Our words seem lifeless. We cannot complete sentences. Rambling is the order of the hour. The airplane of our message appears to be in a holding pattern, circling around and around, unable to find a place to land. And worst of all, those of you who listen to this fiasco unfold are either restlessly fidgeting or simply staring at us with glazed-over looks on your faces! Whether vocalized or not, we can detect the heart cry of some little old lady saying, "Help him, Lord!" And how we long to be helped. And how those of us who've heard such a sermon have longed for the preacher to be helped!

The tragedy of this experience is not its reality, because it's going to happen more often than we would like to think. Flat sermons are just part of the preaching event. The real tragedy is jumping too quickly to the conclusion that such apparent lifelessness is due to the absence of God's spiritual fervor flowing through a man in the preaching event. This premature analysis has led many a pastor to conclude that God's hand is not on his ministry and that he cannot preach with potent power. To say the least, it has bred much discouragement in many of God's beloved shepherds as they have sought to uncover the secret of how God's power is realized in the sermon. Furthermore, it has caused not a few parishioners to give up too quickly on their pastor's preaching.

As the pastor grows confident in the supernatural power of God's Word, however, and adds to his confidence strong convictions about the practice of biblical exposition, he can be certain that the potent power of God will always be in his preaching. Why? The power of God does not rest pragmatically in the preacher but intrinsically in the truth of God's Word. And as we listen to biblical sermons, we can be confident of the same for those who preach to us. As both preacher and people approach the text of Scripture with integrity in preparation, presentation, and reception, the result is sure to be passionate and powerful sermons!

Exalting the Power in the Scriptures

Islam teaches that every Muslim can experience the presence of Allah here and now through the very sounds and syllables of the Arabic Qur'an. Consequently, only the original Arabic is used in prayer, even though most Muslims don't understand it! But it doesn't matter, for they believe the Qur'an was revealed through Muhammad's ears, not his eyes. So, according to Islamic belief, to hear those same words recited and to take them into oneself through prayer is to experience the presence of their god with the greatest degree of intimacy.[1]

For Muslims, at least, there is a relationship between the integrity with which one treats the "oracles of the divine" and the realization of his presence and power. If people place such value on textual integrity in order to access the supposed power and presence of a false god, how much more value should we who worship the one true God place on it when we come to His supernatural Word? Just imagine the extent of Divine presence that can be known when we are completely surrendered to the supernatural sufficiency and authority of God in Scripture! Such is the promise which awaits the preacher and people who align themselves with the potency of the biblical text. Consider these necessities for exalting God's power in Scripture.

Acknowledge the Sufficiency of the Text

If God's Word is our power plant in preaching, then each individual text of Scripture is a potential outlet for plugging into that power. That means the biblical text must be a priority in the pastoral sermon. The potency of pastoral preaching begins, not with the preacher or the perceived needs of the listeners, but with the Bible passage on which the sermon is founded. The use of biblical texts as the foundation for religious discourses has been commonplace since the recognition of a body of inspired Scripture. Since that time the biblical text has been the primary change agent in the preaching event. So obviously it ought to be featured in the sermon.

The great Bible preachers and homileticians of our day continue to affirm the potency of the text of Holy Writ. For example, Bryan Chapell cited the Word as the avenue through which the Holy Spirit impacts us as listeners:

When we proclaim the Word we bring the work of the Holy Spirit to bear on others' lives. No truth grants greater encouragement in our preaching and gives us more cause to expect results from our efforts. The work of the Spirit is as inextricably linked to preaching as heat is to the light a bulb emits. When we present the light of God's Word, his Spirit performs God's purposes of warming, melting, and conforming hearts to his will.[2]

Stowell concurred, specifically identifying the text as the expression of God's Word and calling upon pastors to make it central in their sermons:

The text must be preeminent in our preparation, and preeminent in our presentation. Sermons that deal only lightly and/or obscurely with the text cannot achieve the purpose of bonding people to God and His Word. Nor do they carry the long-term power that is needed to effect life-changing proclamation. Power is not in the clever creations of the communicator but rather in the intrinsic truth of the Word of God through him.[3]

The text-driven sermon is the agent through which the Spirit of God calls people to decision. The biblical text is the only sure foundation for calling people to a changed lifestyle.

The partnership of a prominent biblical text with the Holy Spirit is the key to potent pastoral sermons. Donald Miller described this partnership as "an act wherein the living truth of some portion of Holy Scripture, understood in the light of solid exegetical and historical study and made a living reality to the preacher by the Holy Spirit, comes alive to the hearer as he is confronted by God in Christ through the Holy Spirit in judgment and redemption."[4] Such is the essence of powerful biblical preaching, the only legitimate preaching that will affect listeners. God promised to bless His Word only, not the cleverness or eloquence of the preacher. The text must be a priority in the sermon!

Submit to the Authority of the Text

The supernatural power of God in His Word makes the role of the biblical text in the sermon all important. The word *text* implies a web; thus, the biblical text provides the basic threads with which the sermon is built. It is in the truth of God within the text of Scripture that the supernatural power of God lies. This being the case, the text of Scripture must be preeminent in every pastoral sermon, and the truth of that text must be exposed for listeners to encounter.

The text of Scripture, interpreted rightly and applied with integrity, gives the sermon authority. In the sermon, the pastor's authority does not come primarily in his calling or his position but first and foremost with his passage. And the pastor's perception of authority has direct bearing on his development and delivery of his sermons. As he handles the text of Scripture in preparation and preaching, he must submit himself to the authority of each passage to the greatest degree. Then and only then can those who listen to preaching be expected to offer the same submission.

Homileticians have identified five types of biblical authority in sermons.[5] I want to mention them here in the order of digressing degrees of divine dominion. As you consider the nature of each one, think about two things. First, consider the relationship of each degree of authority with the clarity of God's voice in the sermon. Second, evaluate how each degree of authority relates to the submission of the preacher and the listeners.

A sermon with *direct biblical authority* treats the text of Scripture in accordance with its intended meaning. Building on the natural, grammatical, historical, and theological meaning of the passage, it moves from the *then* to the *now* in a straightforward fashion. This sermon seeks to say the same thing as its text.

A sermon with *indirect biblical authority* uses Scripture in a secondary way, varying from the meaning of the text. Although it may begin with the natural, grammatical, historical *then* of the text, it quickly moves to the *now* at a tangent from the central idea of the passage or passages. This type of sermon is usually weighted with the preacher's expansion and/or reduction of the intent of the text.

Still other sermons contain *casual biblical authority,* making a rather free use of the intended meaning of the text. This type of message usually does not even begin with the historical meaning of the biblical passage and maintains a rather loose relationship with it throughout. About this highly subjective approach that characterized the last century, Brown lamented: "Most likely, more sermons of this type have been preached during the twentieth century than all other types combined. What a tragic commentary on the modern state of preaching! What a shallow regard this demonstrates for the Bible!"[6] The same horror no doubt should be expressed as we analyze sermons at the dawn of the twenty-first century.

The final two types seek either to combine various degrees of the text's authority or even to corrupt it. A sermon with *combination biblical authority* simply uses an integration of any or all of the other types. A sermon with *corrupted biblical authority* cannot even be said to use the biblical text, but instead it abuses it. And countless ways have been discovered for twisting, misusing, and corrupting texts. Obviously these final two types have the potential of overlapping, the latter corrupting the former.

Now here are my questions. Why would any pastor want to adopt a lesser degree of biblical authority when the highest degree is always possible? And why would listeners want to sit under preaching that was not as authoritative as it could be? It is the difference between saying "Thus saith the Lord!" and "Thus suggesteth the Lord!" or "Thus implieth the Lord!" or even "Thus saith the Lord—possibly!" Commenting on the casual biblical sermon, Brown explained:

> A valid question may be asked here. If this sermon represents
> such a weak and inferior use of Scripture, why discuss it in a
> book which seeks to have reformation in preaching? The casual
> sermon must be discussed for two basic reasons: (1) that men
> who use it may see this procedure, with its weaknesses, defined
> and illustrated, and (2) that those who use it may see this form
> in comparison to better forms and thereby be helped in chang-
> ing to better methods and procedures. Those who preach casual
> sermons regularly should strive to move up to direct Biblical
> sermons.[7]

I believe the same question could and should be posed with regard to the indirect, combination, and corrupted sermons. Sermons based upon anything other than direct biblical authority do not carry the highest degree of divine weight and, therefore, fail to be worthy of our submission.

Therein is the link between philosophy and process, between theology and practice, between conviction and form. Just as the pastor's responsibility in preaching flows out of his view of revelation, so his approach to preaching flows out of his view of authority. And the connection between authority and exposition becomes obvious. John Stott wed the two thoughts in reflecting on the practice of the early church:

> We note . . . that the public reading of Scripture came first,
> identifying the authority. What followed was exposition and
> application, whether in the form of doctrinal instruction or of
> moral appeal, or both. Timothy's own authority was thus seen to
> be secondary, both to the Scripture and to the apostle. All
> Christian teachers occupy the same subordinate position as
> Timothy did. They will be wise . . . to demonstrate conscientious

integrity in expounding it, so that their teaching is seen to be not theirs but the word of God.[8]

The pastor's authority as a preacher certainly does not come with a style he copies or an impression he receives. Nor does it come from implications or applications of the intended meaning of a text of Scripture. His authority comes by way of the truth he rightly proclaims. That truth has been revealed by God and should be exposed to people in the most direct way possible.

The most deceptive thing about an analysis of the landscape of contemporary preaching is not the heresy that flows from the pulpits of perverted churches, denominations, and cults. The most deceptive thing is the lesser degrees of biblical authority which undergird the sermons in many conservative pulpits, especially indirect and casual sermons. These are sermons that fail to tap the authority of the text from which they supposedly come.

Think about it. Most of us who know our Bibles to any degree recognize when the biblical text is being contradicted, corrupted, and even ignored. But when the Scriptures are being used indirectly or even casually in sermons, many congregants receive and even applaud them solely because of their incorporation of the Bible, albeit ever so loose. Richard C. White said that these sermons

> are quite readily received and appreciated as Christian preaching. They speak of things conventionally sermonic. They urge a clearly Christian way of life and challenge the hearers to various exemplary enterprises. [They are] quite Christian in content and intent, sound in doctrine, and they may also be compellingly relevant, sensitive to our current situation. In such preaching we hearers are clearly addressed where we live, in specific modern terms. We hear the claim of the gospel.[9]

Yet, in all of this, these kinds of sermons have no biblical authority. They fail to claim the listeners by the eternal truths of the text and the historical realities which encase them. And the tragic result is that man's assumptions and opinions get exalted instead of the reign of God!

We must remember that the role of the pastoral preacher is to exalt God by preaching the Word of God with the highest degree of integrity. The highest degree of integrity comes only with the highest degree of authority. And the only real authoritative preaching is biblical exposition where the preacher and listeners are in submission to the primary meaning of each text. That's where we find *God's stuff*, not just *good stuff!* When the preacher allows the text to be preeminent, people are sure to be getting *God's stuff!* And when they get His stuff, He gets the glory!

Extracting the Power in the Study

While it may not seem very academic and polished, the preaching approach practiced by one elderly country preacher still serves as the best way for the pastor to prepare. When asked how he prepared to preach, the wise minister replied: "First, I reads myself full; then, I prays myself hot; then, I lets go!" I believe that's a pretty good description of how a preacher goes about tapping into the power of God—reading, praying, and letting go!

While the power of God lies exclusively in His Word and not in His preacher, the Father has graciously chosen for the two to be wed together for effective preaching. And the wedding of God's Word and God's preacher takes place in two secluded places—the study and the prayer closet. If you want the Holy Spirit to come upon you in great power, you will need to engage His inspired Word through faithful preparation and fervent prayer. To these two places the pastor must steal away in order to extract God's supernatural power from His Word and enable it to come alive in his heart.

Vitalize the Message in the Closet

The wedding of text and preacher for powerful preaching ultimately takes place in the prayer closet. While the Word of God is innately living and powerful, it is only vitalized in the preacher's heart through unhurried prayer. E. M. Bounds said that God's power "comes to the preacher not in the study but in the closet."[10] Consequently, prayer must permeate the preparation process—before, during, and after the intellectual aspects of study are engaged.

To shepherd God's people through preaching is an incredibly awesome task. Some preachers may think they can shortcut the expositional process by downloading good sermons off of the Internet, but they will never be able to download the power of God except through unhurried, isolated, and sacrificial prayer regarding the preaching task. Preacher, cry out to God and ask the Spirit to infuse His Word into your heart! Parishioner, cry out to God on behalf of your shepherd who is seeking to hear from God and be clothed in His power!

Pastor, after you have prayerfully selected a preaching text, pray over the passage in several ways. First, pray for illumination as you read the text. The Holy Spirit will illuminate your mind and assist you in understanding what you read. Second, pray the text for yourself as you begin to glean what the Holy

Spirit is saying in the passage. The pastor preaches most powerfully on truths which have first been applied to his own life. Third, pray the text for those who will listen to you preach it. It has rightly been said, "The preacher who has never learned in the school of Christ the high and divine act of intercession for his people will never learn the art of preaching, though homiletics be poured into him by the ton, and though he be the most gifted genius in sermon-making and sermon delivery."[11]

Praying over your preaching text heightens sermon potency in three ways. First, it helps you to internalize and personalize the truth that you will proclaim. You will own it and, therefore, proclaim it with a hot heart! Second, it helps you to identify the text with your listeners from the outset of your preparation. You will be helping them to own it before they even hear it! Third, it engages you in the most powerful kind of praying—that which is according to the will of God. When you pray Scripture, you always pray according to the will of God. And "this is the confidence that we have in Him, that if we ask anything according to His will, He hears us" (1 John 5:14)!

Dearly beloved pastor and people, understand one more thing before we leave this subject. Please know that you will not always experience God's power in equal measure in every sermon. For reasons known only to God, sometimes the Spirit will fall and at other times the sermon will fall flat. If the pastor has sought the Lord diligently in prayer, it's not ours to determine why. It's simply ours to bathe God's Word, His shepherds, and our lives in prayer, and then to leave the outcome in His sovereign hands. That way He gets the glory. So tarry long in praying over your passage and your pastor.

Verify the Meaning by Consensus

Several years ago one of the great Bible expositors of our day was teaching in a pastor's training school on the value of using various Bible study tools for sermon preparation. During a discussion time a young man posed an important question to him. "Sir," he asked, "don't you think it's important for me just to get alone with God and find out what the Holy Spirit is saying to me?" The preacher's answer was shocking. "Young man," he replied, "I'm not interested in what the Holy Spirit is saying to *you*. In fact, you may be surprised to know that I'm not interested in what the Holy Spirit is saying to *me*." Then he explained. "All I'm interested in is what the Holy Spirit is *saying*, and the Holy Spirit has been saying the same thing through a passage of Scripture since the day He inspired it. And I'm going to use every available means that I have to find out what that is."

This kind of commitment beckons the pastor to add intellectual preparation to his praying in order to extract God's power from the text of Scripture. And diligent preparation is the responsibility of the pastor who sets out to remove the sedimentary layers that have covered God's revelation over the years. It is the task of the one who would venture to expose the truth of God's Word through *every available means*! Some have dared to suggest that all the preacher needs in order to be faithful to the task are his Bible and the Holy Spirit. But many fail to remember that the mind of the Holy Spirit is found on the pages of the inspired text, a text whose right meaning has been covered up over time with layers of various languages, backgrounds, settings, time periods, and the like. Consequently, the faithful "exposer" of truth must use *every available means* to uncover the layers and discover the mind of the Holy Spirit.

Diligent and careful preparation enables the expositor to interpret the biblical text with integrity. Furthermore, integrity demands that the preacher verify his conclusions regarding the meaning of the text. We must always remember that we—as human vessels—are the fallible and errant part of the hermeneutical process. God's Word is inerrant and infallible; we are not. Therefore, it becomes our responsibility to minimize our role along the hermeneutical journey to the greatest degree. Because we want to be as objective as possible in our study of the Bible, we must work to reduce our subjectivity. And tweaking Bounds's contention, it could be said that minimal subjectivity "comes to the preacher not in the closet but in the study."

Consequently, textual integrity will only be maintained as the pastor logs unhurried seat time with what we will call the *dead preachers society* of his library. While all of the authors he consults will not be deceased, their works do form a society within which the pastor can do good biblical hermeneutics. This society should be made up of commentators, linguists, Bible scholars, historians, and many others who have gone before us in the study of Scripture and who have made their findings available in written form. Their works will guide the expositor to consider issues like grammar and syntax, biblical context, cultural and historical background, and biblical and systematic theology. Minimizing the subjectivity of the interpreter requires us to surround ourselves with a team of individuals to hold the preacher accountable. Such accountability is best arrived at by consensus.

The diligent expositor can never be so arrogant as to think that he has the corner on the market when it comes to understanding truth. Instead, he must humbly lay his own insights alongside those of other godly servants in order to make an honest assessment of every given passage of Scripture. Regarding the meaning of words, phrases, and verses, he must be serious enough to ask, "Where does the weight of the evidence lie?" At times the preacher will glean insight into Scripture that few, if any, writers before him have discovered. But those times will be the exceptions and not the rule. In most cases and with most passages, the consensus—or majority—opinion of the hermeneutical society will bring the meaning of words, phrases, verses, and ideas to the surface where they can be clearly seen. The preacher who determines to treat the text with integrity must be willing to submit his own ideas, and even his own sermons, to the verdict of the group.

Expressing the Power in the Sermon

Of the three primary factors that influenced the development of Christian preaching—ancient oratory and rhetoric, Hebrew prophecy, and the Christian gospel—the gospel was the primary originating cause because it gave preaching its content. As principles of rhetoric were later applied, preachers began to employ ways of convincing and persuading persons to respond to the gospel. But the gospel itself is where the real power rests. As men, women, boys, and girls hear Scripture and respond to it in faith, the power of the gospel is applied for salvation and spiritual transformation. Consequently, teaching pastors and listening people must take great pains to ensure that the passage of inspired Scripture is exalted in sermon. Here's how we can do it.

Let the Text Be Seen

The scene is quite humbling. Two hundred people are packed inside an unofficial Chinese house church, the only one—legal or illegal—in the village. Four hundred more jam the narrow alley outside, many with their ears pressed up against a wall or listening via a makeshift speaker to the preaching of the Bible inside. While the government of China allows some "legal" Bibles in their country, it's not nearly enough for growing Christian families or new converts. Even the legal Bibles are often confiscated by the police. Millions of people in China have lived a long life and died without ever seeing a Bible or hearing God's Word. The same scenario is repeated every week all across the globe. In some Muslim nations like Bangladesh, Christians with Bibles are burned with cigarettes. In Saudi Arabia, believers are expelled in chains from the country. People in North Korea have been jailed or put to death for having a Bible.

These realities shame the apparent de-emphasis of the "presence" of the Bible in some worship services in America and other parts of the free world. It's almost like some churches are apologizing for even including it. Several years ago a colleague commented that because many people had stopped bringing their Bibles to church, he had stopped opening his when he got up to preach. God forbid! We hear a lot about biblical illiteracy today and the fact that we live in an oral culture. These realities have led many preachers and churches to at best downplay the physical presence of the Bible in preaching and worship. Some even see it as a hindrance. Smaller Bibles, phrases lifted from the text and printed on a screen or handout, and—worst of all—unopened Bibles left on the pew or pulpit speak volumes to observant listeners.

I believe we ought to make the Bible visible in our preaching and worship. There's not any one particular way to go about doing this, but we need to be intentional about it. If you want to talk about biblical illiteracy, Ezra and Nehemiah lived in a scripturally illiterate and oral culture. And the way they responded was to make the physical scroll as visible as possible. And that speaks volumes about value! When Ezra opened the scroll to teach the people, "he stood on a platform of wood which they had made for the purpose;" he did it "in the sight of all the people" (Neh. 8:4–5).

Some churches today are making efforts to enhance the speaker-audience relationship by removing pulpits, communion furniture, and even putting the preacher down on the same level as the congregation. None of those are hills I'm willing to die on, but we do need to give consideration to the reasons some stuff was used in the first place. Platforms elevated the speaker and made the word more visible and audible. Pulpits gave preachers a place to set their Bibles and their teaching notes, highlighting the centrality of the Word in worship at the same time. Family Bibles on communion tables in front of pulpits under-scored the place of the Scriptures in the community of faith. If you take the symbols away, friend, make sure you replace them with other intentional efforts toward making the Bible visible in preaching and worship.

One of the first things I did when I started pastoring the church I now serve was to meet with the choir. No, I didn't try to tell them how to sing or which robes to wear. I simply asked them to be sure to always bring their Bibles into the choir loft, to always open them when I got up to preach, and to at least look like they were following along. Why? Because choirs members are worship leaders, and that visible picture is worth a thousand words to the congregation when it comes to the importance of the Bible.

I realize that one of these days it may very well be illegal in this country to have a Bible in public. Some of the civil rights rulings being handed down today seem to suggest that's a very real possibility. But right now it's not illegal. And

I believe that believers—especially in corporate worship—ought to do everything in their power to showcase the Scriptures. Pastors, of all people, ought to bring them into the pulpit—and use them! Our kids ought to see us carrying our Bibles to church, opening them up when the preacher gets up to preach, and following along as he teaches. Every person whose shadow darkens the platform ought to have Bible in hand as an object lesson to the people who are being led in worship.

One thing some pastors and churches are doing in an effort to make the Bible visible is to put the Scripture text up on a screen. While this effort is to be commended, the detriment needs to be noted. It is possible that the easy accessibility of the text subtly encourages listeners not to open their own Bibles or even not to bring them. As one who has devoted his life to encouraging the magnification of the Scriptures in the preaching and teaching ministries, I'm a stickler when it comes to my kids taking their Bibles to church. A while back I noticed my two boys climbing in our vehicle without their Bibles as we prepared to go to midweek services. When I reminded them, they responded by telling me they didn't need them because the youth pastor always put the passage up on the screen! Maybe pew Bibles or extra copies are better options for ensuring that everyone can see the text.

We also need to give serious attention to ensuring that other aspects of the listening environment are right for hearing the Word. So preachers and other church leaders need to give attention to logistical matters. Nothing is worse than for a wonderful sermon or lesson to be drowned in an inadequate sound system, poor lighting, blocked views, distracting platform decor, or any number of other physical circumstances. Give some consideration to the preaching or teaching atmosphere. While it's certainly not the most important issue, it doesn't need to be neglected.

We don't need to make too big a deal out of this, but in light of what has been said previously regarding making the Bible visible, I think it's important for pastors to read their text instead of just "bottom lining" it. It's very important for people to make the connection between what the preacher says about each passage and what the people know to be the authoritative document. Even in a biblically illiterate, postmodern culture, there still is enough credence, though it may be just token, given to the Bible that it merits showing people where you get your explanations and applications. It's an authority issue, so read the text even if the listeners are not looking at it! Making this connection is the beginning point of explanation and right understanding.

The same thing should be said with regard to quoting the preaching text from memory during the sermon. All of us should be in the habit of memorizing Scripture, and the pastor who memorizes his preaching passage is to be commended. But while quoting the text instead of reading it wows a lot of listeners, it probably does more to overwhelm them and distract their attention from looking at their personal copy of God's Word. Again, this is not a right or wrong issue, but the trade-offs probably weigh more toward the benefit of reading the text even when it's been memorized.

All of these issues and more go a long way to show the importance of the Bible in corporate worship. And they also do much to heighten the chances that sermons are heard and heeded. The value that both pastors and listeners place on God's Word will command attention. Preachers need to pay attention to whether or not their listeners are paying attention. We hear much about the shortened attention spans of today's listeners. At best, those claims are overrated and often used as excuses for laziness in preparation, presentation, and reception. Church worship services seem to be just about the only place that people claim short attention. Don't be fooled! If the preacher gives people something, they'll stay with him. And when you combine hard work with the Word of God and a spirit-filled preacher, attention spans will have a way of growing!

Take the Listeners for a Swim

Not only do we need to make the text visible in corporate worship; we need to go swimming in it! The process of exposition plays out in the sermon as the preacher presents, explains, and expounds facts or ideas with commentary and interpretation. This is the very heart of the pastoral sermon. As the pastor engages the listeners with the text of the Bible, he exposes them to the only thing that possesses the ability to change their lives. Picturing the sermon as a body of water, I have often likened this engagement to the activity that goes on in a backyard swimming pool. Let me clarify the implications with regard to the types of biblical authority mentioned earlier.

As I see it, there are basically three ways a pastor can use the text of Scripture in his sermon. Many preachers use the text merely as a diving board in their sermons. They jump off of the text into the sermon, swim around for twenty to forty minutes, and never return to it. They read a passage at the beginning of the message and then never mention it again! Still other preachers treat the text like patio furniture around the pool. They swim around in the sermon but make only casual and periodic visits to the text. Just as the pool furniture is there to augment the pool, these pastors actually are using the text of the Bible to augment their sermons, almost as illustrative or supportive material.

In reality, the text simply does not happen in these sermons. The preacher announces and reads the text, assumes it to be authoritative because it comes from the Bible, and then proceeds to reduce it to a theme. The only time the text is revisited is for the purpose of repetition or for springboarding off of another loose reference. White described the snowball affect:

> Now, possessed of the "theme" . . . the preacher gets down to the serious business of "developing" and "applying" the theme. After all, the theme is short and pithy, implying a lot in a few general words. But the sermon must spell out at length, develop, and explain what's implied in it. And what does the preacher use for this development? What authority does the sermon invoke in support of its "theme"? Why, every authoritative source the preacher knows and can find—except the lesson on which the sermon is being preached.[12]

The real problem here is a lack of confidence in the sufficiency of the biblical text. The preacher has abandoned his belief that the Scripture passage has anything to offer, nor does he believe it possesses the power to transform lives. Digesting its content into the "theme," he prostitutes the potent Word of God for the observations, conjectures, and experiences of man.

Many of these kinds of sermons—heard weekly from pulpits and platforms across the globe—are based on the indirect, casual, or combined biblical authority we discussed earlier. Many more are even corrupted. And even the best of these is void of the total strength and full authority of Scripture possessed by the biblical sermon. Therefore, these sermons are weaker and less potent than direct biblical sermons.

The expositor, however, uses the text of Scripture as the pool itself. He jumps off into it and goes for a swim. In this message the text is actually the sermon, and the preaching pastor is allowing it to be the main event. He and his listeners are being immersed in the supernatural, life-changing agent of God's Holy Word. This pastor gives the text a real voice in the sermon. The primary feature of the sermon, then, is a journey into the biblical text where the preacher immerses both himself and his listeners in a rhetorical presentation of a Bible passage. Then and only then does the preacher tap into the full authority and the full potency of the biblical text.

Swimming in the text often means translating the languages of the Bible into the language of the people. As I mentioned in chapter 4, the Jews would have used Aramaic while in captivity because it was the international diplomatic language of the day much like English is in our day. Consequently, part of the work of the Levites when "they gave the sense" (Neh. 8:8) was to give the people an Aramaic translation of the Hebrew text. But "translation" always involves more than just moving from one language to another. All translations involve interpretation to some degree. And that's what preachers and teachers do—they interpret the Scriptures for the people by breaking it up paragraph by paragraph.

Essentially, swimming in the text means "exposing" the people to God's intended meaning of each text that has been covered up by language, time, culture, social setting, and many other factors. That's the responsibility of the contemporary Christian communicator. Your primary responsibility is not to give opinions, indirect implications, or extrabiblical principles but instead to expose the Holy Spirit's intended meaning in each passage of Scripture so that people's minds are exposed to supernatural truth and their lives are transformed into the image of Jesus Christ. You are to translate it into the vernacular of the people to whom you speak. This kind of interaction with the text is at the very heart of biblical exposition and is the beginning point of life transformation. With two disciples on the road to Emmaus, "beginning at Moses and all the Prophets, [Jesus] expounded to them in all the Scriptures the things concerning Himself. . . . And they said to one another, 'Did not our heart burn within us while He talked with us on the road, and while He opened the Scriptures to us?'" (Luke 24:27, 32). God's Word, rightly understood, does something to the human heart!

Based upon my own personal observation, the most effective musical worship leaders are not those men and women who stand before a crowd of people and guide the musicians and congregation in praise with precision and skillful mechanics. The most effective musical worship leaders are those who enter into worship themselves and then simply invite the rest of us to join in with them. There is something authentic and meaningful about such a journey. In the same manner, the most effective preaching pastors are not those who get up before their people and present a sermonic creation with homiletical skill and oratorical precision. The most effective preaching pastors are those who dive into a passage of Scripture and then beckon their listeners to join them for a swim. That is a life-changing journey!

Don't ever forget that spiritual transformation is rooted in the power of proclaimed Scripture combined with the work of the Holy Spirit, not in your own skill and giftedness as a preacher or a student of God's Word. Without a doubt, expository sermons are the most effective way to subject people to this supernatural, life-changing combination. Much of today's preaching prompts little more than a sleepy nod, much less life change. Through the exposition of texts of Scripture, God encounters individuals to draw them to salvation and Christian maturity.

Where Do I Go from Here . . .

Now that you have completed this look at the practical aspects of the theology of pastoral preaching, you may proceed one of two ways as indicated by the shaded areas on the chart below. The (▼) symbol indicates the thematic development of the remainder of these practical implications. If you are following this path, proceed to chapter 9, "Preaching for Eternity." If you are following the development of thought from biblical to philosophical to practical, you have finished consideration of the *resource* for pastoral preaching and can now begin to look at the *goal*. If you are following this path, go back to chapter 3, "The Motive in Preaching."

Table 8.1

	PART 1 **(Biblical)**		**PART 2** **(Philosophical)**		**PART 3** **(Practical)**
(Content)	Chapter 1: The Message of Preaching ▼	➡	Chapter 4: The Shepherd's Stewardship ▼	➡	Chapter 7: Preaching as Worship ▼
(Resource)	Chapter 2: The Means for Preaching ▼	➡	Chapter 5: The Shepherd's Power ▼	➡	Chapter 8: Preaching with Potency ▼
(Goal)	Chapter 3: The Motive in Preaching	➡	Chapter 6: The Shepherd's Relevance	➡	Chapter 9: Preaching for Eternity

CHAPTER 9

Preaching for Eternity:
KINGDOM RELAY

Although it was not my favorite sport, I ran track in high school mainly to stay in shape for football. I ran what is now the killer 800-meter run, then the 880-yard dash, because I had pretty good endurance but no blazing speed. But I was always envious of the guys who ran the relay races, especially the sprint relay. I thought it was so cool the way they worked as a team in passing the baton as they moved around the track.

As faith communities are developed under the exposition of God's Word, they have a responsibility to replicate themselves in subsequent generations. In his second letter to the young pastor, the apostle Paul reminded Timothy that he was part of a kingdom relay race, and the baton was the Word of God which had been entrusted to him. Paul said that his forefathers began the race by handing him the baton (see 2 Tim. 1:3). He in turn had passed it to Lois and Eunice, Timothy's grandmother and mother respectively, who then passed it on to Paul's young protégé (see 2 Tim. 1:5). One of the major reasons Paul wrote this letter was to encourage Timothy—who apparently was timid and ready to quit—to stay in the race and pass the baton to the next generation. That is why he challenges the timid shepherd with these words: "And the things that you have heard from me among many witnesses, commit these to faithful men who will be able to teach others also" (2 Tim. 2:2). This kingdom relay requires the contemporary church both to carry the baton today and then sufficiently pass it to the church of tomorrow.

Holding on to the Baton

The interesting thing I discovered about the relay race is that the winning team is not the one whose last runner crosses the finish line first. The winning team in the relay race is the team whose last runner crosses the finish line first *with the baton*. And any team that drops the baton and has to take the time to pick it up is sure to lose. So it is with the heritage of Christian doctrine. If we mishandle our biblical faith, we will be unable to deliver it adequately to those who come behind us.

At the risk of saying the obvious, heretical teachers and errant religious groups intentionally drop the baton of the faith in our day in efforts to impede the spread of the gospel. But we must realize that many evangelical pastors who insist on delivering to their listeners *good stuff* instead of *God's stuff* also are allowing the baton to fall to the track. And the congregations who expect such sermonizing are guilty of the same. Consider some ways to maintain a firm grip.

Promote Biblical Literacy

I've often likened the present state of the church to that of the pharaoh in Egypt regarding Joseph after his death. The penman of the Pentateuch noted that "there arose a new king over Egypt, who did not know Joseph" (Ex. 1:8). The problem of the pharaoh—and the subsequent problem of the children of Israel—was that he didn't know the Joseph through whom God had chosen to bless His people. Our problem—and the subsequent problem of the generations which will follow us—is that we don't know the Joseph of basic Christian doctrine through which God has chosen to develop and nurture faith communities. Calvin Miller grieved:

> More and more, we are unable to locate the visible doctrinal
> church of Christ. In the current salad bar, mix-and-match of
> church program and community activities, many theologians are
> growing concerned that the church is losing the ability to define
> and defend its faith. What does the church believe, and why
> does it believe? What are its tenets and why?[1]

Truly, when it comes to preservation of the Christian faith and the communities it shapes, we're raising a generation that knows not Joseph!

It appears that Jude expressed a similar concern to the early church saying, "I found it necessary to write to you exhorting you to contend earnestly for the faith which was once for all delivered to the saints" (Jude 3). As noted in chapter 3, this one faith is the content of the gospel in its complete form and is equivalent to God's revealed and recorded Word, the Bible. Here again the practice of biblical exposition rises to the surface as the need of the hour. Not every hermeneutical process and not every sermonic form is conducive to preserving and teaching the principles of the faith that have been delivered to the saints. Only through solid, expository preaching can pastors and people turn the tide of spiritual ignorance and complacent Christianity. The following actions should provide some motivation for fighting for the faith and developing a consciousness that will never again forget Joseph.

Not long ago I remember watching a segment on a television show that would have been hilarious if it were not so tragic. Jay Leno, host of NBC's *The Tonight Show*, went out on the streets of Hollywood to question unsuspecting passersby about the Bible. His questions were not hard; in fact, they were designed to be easy. That is where the laughs—and the tears—came in. Leno asked with a twinkle in his eye, "Name one of the Ten Commandments." Answer: "God helps those who help themselves." The audience laughed. Leno asked someone else, "Can you name one of the apostles?" There was no reply. He continued, "OK, then name the four Beatles." Immediate response: "George, Paul, John and Ringo." The crowd cheered. Leno moved on to another victim and said, "Can you tell me, according to the Bible, who was swallowed by a great fish?" Answer: "Pinocchio." The audience roared. The bit continued, and it only got worse.

If you think the scenario was staged, listen to what one prominent research group recently discovered:

> Only one out of four Americans can correctly identify John 3:16.
> Only one out of five Americans can correctly define the gospel.
> Only one out of three Americans read their Bible regularly.
> Only one out of three Americans believe in a literal hell.
> Only one out of ten Americans can identify the Great Commission.
> Four out of ten Americans cannot name half of the Ten
> Commandments.
> Four out of ten Americans cannot name one of the four Gospels.
> Four out of ten Americans believe that Jesus sinned.

If your church members, youth group, student ministry council, or your own children were visiting Hollywood and just happened to be walking outside the NBC studio when Jay Leno took his roving mike to the streets, how would they fare? Would their answers fall to the cutting room floor, or would they be so far off the wall that they would make late-night TV? How well does the generation for which we are responsible really know the Bible?

Paul told Timothy, his young pastor friend, that remaining faithful to his heritage would require good stewardship of God's Word, that which had been entrusted—or *deposited*—to him in his own generation. He wrote:

> Hold fast the pattern of sound words which you have heard
> from me, in faith and love which are in Christ Jesus. That good
> thing which was committed to you, keep by the Holy Spirit who
> dwells in us (2 Tim. 1:13–14).

These two verses contain two sets of parallel descriptions of this stewardship that magnify the importance of promoting biblical literacy in our day with integrity, intentionality, diligence, care, and accountability.

First, Paul describes the deposit as the "pattern of sound words" and the "good thing." The word *pattern* is the word used in the language of the New Testament of a writer's outline or an artist's rough sketch. It refers to something that sets the guidelines and standards for the finished work. This standard is further described as being "of sound words." The word *sound* means "healthy, or health giving." "Good" denotes that which is intrinsically good as opposed to that which is good in its benefit. Put it all together and what you have is that the believer's "pattern" for spiritual health is the Bible, God's own truth and standards. It is the only divinely inspired and sufficient truth containing everything necessary for salvation and for living out the saved life. And the nutritionist-shepherd has been given the responsibility to dispense it.

Second, Paul charges the young shepherd to "hold fast" and to "keep" this standard. Together these words convey the idea of adhering to and guarding the thing that has been entrusted. All believers—but especially God's shepherds—have been entrusted with the very treasure of God, the Holy Scriptures. It is a sacred trust that carries with it high stakes and magnifies the responsibility of both pastor and people to guard it with their lives. Such is the challenge today. As we face the onslaught of biblical illiteracy, shepherds especially must give themselves to changing the tide, for the sake of the current generation as well as those that follow. Like Timothy, pastors today must remain faithful to our heritage by systematically teaching and preaching the doctrine that has been entrusted to us. And we who listen to sermons must demand it.

Chuck Swindoll, speaking at a recent graduation ceremony at Liberty University, said that the greatest need in our times is for God's people to be biblically literate. If you want to talk about the needs of people, this one is huge. And it's our responsibility to meet it. Someone has said that the influence of the Bible on our society is fading faster than a California sunset. It has indeed become the world's best-selling coffee-table book. In our anti-authoritarian, post-Christian, techno-world, many consider the Bible a useless collection of myths and legends. So it suffers from benign neglect, which may prove not to be benign at all. The room for improvement in knowing what the Bible says, understanding what it means, applying it to our everyday lives, and protecting it for the next generation is the biggest room in the world. And it will take both shepherd and sheep to change it.

Preserve Pastoral Responsibility

One of the biggest challenges in fighting for the faith today is the need to preserve the biblical role of the pastor. To do that, both pastor and people will need to reform the modern expectations regarding the pastoral office. Many shepherds are unable to fulfill their biblical responsibilities because of the redefinition that has taken place about what a pastor is and does.

In chapter 4 we noted that Christ invested two offices—evangelists and pastor-teachers—in the church to guide it into the likeness of Jesus Christ (see Eph. 4:11–16). These gifted men, who are themselves gifts to the church, have been supplied with two primary tools with which they are to equip the saints for service so that the body can be built up. These supernatural resources are prayer and the ministry of God's Word. Like the apostles in Jerusalem, the shepherd is to give himself above all else to these two activities (see Acts 6:4).

Through prayer, the pastor-teacher indirectly equips the saints for works of service, which in turn edifies the body. On his knees, he prepares himself and leads his people to prepare themselves for spiritual service. Epaphras obviously was committed to this spiritual means of growing believers, for Paul told the Colossian believers that he was "always laboring fervently for you in prayers, that you may stand *perfect and complete* in all the will of God" (Col. 4:12, emphasis added). Prayer is the slender nerve that moves the muscle of omnipotence in accomplishing His re-creative work in the lives of His people!

Through God's inspired Word, the Bible, the shepherd directly equips the saints for works of service. Through the preaching and teaching of the Scriptures, he resources his flock "for doctrine, for reproof, for correction, for instruction in righteousness, that the man of God may be *complete*, thoroughly equipped for every good work" (2 Tim. 3:16–17, emphasis added). It is interesting to note that when Paul wrote to Timothy, who was a pastor in Ephesus, about equipping the saints for the work of the ministry, he did it in the context of a discussion about the effectualness of the Scriptures. We are on safe ground, then, to assume he had the same equipping agent in mind when he wrote to the Ephesians earlier in his ministry. As the shepherd preaches and teaches the Bible, he shapes people into Christ's image.

The connection between *equipping* and the *Scriptures* and *growth* is even more direct in the Ephesians passage mentioned above. The ultimate target of Christlikeness in church growth begins with "the unity of the faith" (Eph. 4:13). And this faith is not fragmented or divided against itself. Whenever a church is fragmented and divided, it simply means the people are to some degree apart from a right knowledge and understanding of His truth. But when they are biblically equipped with doctrinal integrity, faithfully serving, and spiritually maturing, then and only then will they "come to the unity of the faith and of the knowledge of the Son of God, to a perfect man, to the measure of the stature of the fullness of Christ" (Eph. 4:13). So essentially the right teaching of God's Word is the launching pad for maturing the body into Christlikeness.

By default, the need or doctrinal integrity designates the pastor as the church's "resident theologian." Along with his responsibility of heightening the flock's biblical literacy, he is charged with the task of teaching them right theology. As Elizabeth Achtemeier observed, the teaching pastor

> has the task of educating the congregation in the central beliefs of Christianity. . . . For far too long we have turned the responsibility for Christian education over to the Sunday school, with mixed results. Long before there was a Sunday school, faithful clergy taught their congregations Christian theology in their Sunday sermons, and traditional Christian theology has been preserved in the church.[2]

As the congregation's church theologian, the pastor is charged with the responsibility of guarding and teaching the church's understanding about God. Such an awesome responsibility beckons the shepherd to give diligent time and attention to the task.

If the preacher is faithful and obedient to the Holy Spirit to "command and teach" the truth of God's Word (1 Tim. 3:11), then he "will be a good minister of Jesus Christ, nourished in the words of faith and of the good doctrine" (1 Tim. 4:6). Paul underscored the supremacy of this task in the pastor's ministry when he sternly charged young Timothy to

> give attention to reading, to exhortation, to doctrine. Do not neglect the gift that is in you, which was given to you by prophecy with the laying on of the hands of the eldership. Meditate on these things; give yourself entirely to them, that your progress may be evident to all. Take heed to yourself and

> to the doctrine. Continue in them, for in doing this you will save
> both yourself and those who hear you (1 Tim. 4:13–16).

Obviously, Paul is speaking here of the ability of God's Word to deliver from the bondage of the flesh. That's what happens when the pastor faithfully exposes the truth of the Bible.

We already know why Paul's charges are so important. It's because "the time will come when they will not endure sound doctrine, but according to their own desires, because they have itching ears, they will heap up for themselves teachers; and they will turn their ears away from the truth, and be turned aside to fables" (2 Tim. 4:3–4). It would be easy to write Paul's reference here off as simply the heretical teaching that characterizes liberal churches and even cults today. But don't miss it, beloved! Paul's words here include warm fuzzy "faiths" that characterize much conservative preaching, and it's already the order of our day!

Practically, all this means the stakes are high regarding pastoral responsibility and priority. Contemporary pastors are going to have to shun the modern model of CEO management and return to the apostolic responsibilities of prayer and study if they are to preserve the biblical role. This does not mean the shepherd is relieved of other pastoral duties. But it does mean that he will have to exercise the ministry of planned neglect, planning to neglect some things in order to prioritize others. His Palm Pilot or DayTimer will need to reflect his prioritization of his primary biblical responsibilities. And the faithful congregation who hungers to hear the voice of God on Sundays must rise to help their shepherd protect his time for prayer and preaching preparation during the week.

Handing off the Baton

Besides carrying the baton securely, the faithful relay runner has still another responsibility—the smooth delivery of the baton to the next member of the team. In relay races, the exchanges of the baton between members of the team are critical. Sloppy, ill-timed transfers can cause a team to lose even a hundredth of a second, which easily can be the difference between winning and losing.

The exchanges of the Christian faith via faithful exposition of God's Word certainly have faced numerous challenges throughout history. Yet the resilience of the runners provides great inspiration and encouragement for those who would take up the mantle in our day. Dear preacher and listeners, consider the

Author and Finisher of the race, as well as those who have run the legs in between!

Remember Your Roots

Our faithfulness in passing the baton begins with remembering that expository preaching has its roots in the One who was with the Father from the beginning. Without apology we will admit that we have no way of knowing if Jesus Christ was an expository preacher in the same vein I have been discussing. We've already discussed some important distinctions between His role as a preacher and the role of contemporary preachers that help us to reconcile that issue (see chapter 4). At the same time, it is helpful to consider the Master's ministry when thinking about the heritage of exposition from eternity past.

The mandate of biblical exposition given to contemporary preachers is rooted more in the *person* of Jesus than in the *preaching* of Jesus. We are told in John's Gospel that while "no one has seen God . . . the only begotten Son, who is in the bosom of the Father, He has declared Him" (John 1:18). The word *declared* here is the word from which we get our word *exegesis*. It means to "lead out" or "draw out." In other words, Jesus is the divine exegete! In the same way that we exegete a text of Scripture in order to expose its true meaning, the one who was from the beginning exegeted the Father and exposed His true meaning. This means that Jesus was not just *an* expositor; He is *the* expositor! He was not just one among many expositors *in* history; He is the Master-Expositor *of* history! The very nature of the Lord Jesus means that teaching pastors today have their roots in eternity past, and those roots demand they be expositors of who God is and what He says. The heritage of exposition is lashed more to Jesus' holistic function than in His sermon form. Jesus is the one who came out of the blocks with the baton of the Bible.

At the same time, I grow weary of hearing people suggest that contemporary pastoral sermons should not necessarily be expositional because, they say, Jesus did not preach that way. He was the quintessential storyteller, we are reminded, and consequently His approach should be the pattern for modern-day homiletics. They further champion for the bulk of our preaching to be in story form in light of the vast treasury of narrative material which monopolizes biblical literary genre and is the very nature of the four Gospels themselves. Still others contend that few, if any, of the sermons recorded in the Bible can be categorized as expository. These suggestions are shortsighted at best, and they communicate a serious misunderstanding of the nature of pastoral preaching today.

As heretical as it may seem to some, Jesus is not necessarily the best model for contemporary pastoral preaching. This obviously is not because of any flaw in His homiletic or His theology. Certainly Jesus was the quintessential master communicator and the general model for all preachers of all time. However, we must recognize the fact that He did not practice as the preaching pastor of a local congregation in the same vein as we know the ministry today. His ministry would better serve as a model for itinerant preaching as He engaged different crowds in various settings. Additionally, the content of the majority of His preaching and teaching would more closely parallel evangelistic proclamation as opposed to the edification of believers. Besides all this, Jesus' mission on earth was not to provide an example for pastoral preaching but to die for the sins of humanity.

As much as some would like to ignore it, however, the practice of exposition was part of the repertoire of Jesus' proclamation ministry. In one sense, segments of the Sermon on the Mount have an expositional flavor as Jesus referenced what the people had been taught and then proceeded to clarify the intended meaning of each principle (cf. Matt. 5:21–48). His numerous references to Old Testament passages suggest an intent upon clarifying the intended meaning of each one. On the road to Emmaus, He obviously displayed His practice of exposition for, "beginning at Moses and all the Prophets, He expounded to them in all the Scriptures the things concerning Himself" (Luke 24:27). While these references alone do not indicate that Jesus was an expositor as we know the term, they do eliminate the notion that all He did was go around telling stories.

Follow Your Forefathers

Our faithfulness to the relay task continues as we follow in the influence of our forefathers in the faith. Like most of us, I know people whose families are characterized by high blood pressure, high cholesterol, or some other ailing medical condition. Still others I know have less serious qualities like a short stature, a full head of hair, or a big nose. Regardless of the seriousness of the condition, many of these conditions are believed to be hereditary. Their great grandparents had it, their parents had it, and chances are good that their kids will have it. It has been genetically transmitted from parent to offspring in succession. And in most cases, there is nothing a person can do about it. It is simply in the genes.

One of the interesting things about hereditary conditions is that they do not necessarily show up in every generation. The condition may skip a generation or two and then randomly pop up again in the next one. Those are recessive genes. Many critics through the ages have tried to downplay the importance of expository sermons based upon the fact that they have not shown up in every generation, in every place. Still today numerous critics write exposition off as an out-of-date form or, at best, simply categorize it as one of many choices among homiletical approaches. Yet they have failed to recognize exposition's hereditary quality. They have failed to understand that, although recessive at times, it has been in the genes of our forefathers throughout history. Just because it does not show up in every generation or in every preacher or even in every sermon does not negate the heritage that contemporary pastors are responsible for carrying on. It is in the genes of pastoral preaching, and we cannot deny it for the sake of lesser approaches.

For example, the genes of exposition continued to show up after Jesus in apostolic preaching. The Pauline epistles are riddled with implications that such was the conviction in the early church. As has already been noted, Paul instructed young Timothy to "give attention to reading, to exhortation, to doctrine" (1 Tim. 4:13). The foundational exposition of Old Testament Scripture in early synagogue worship gave way to the practice of the early church wherein a public reading from the Old Testament or the apostolic writings was followed by an exposition of the same. Regarding this pattern, Stott strongly asserted that "it was taken for granted from the beginning that Christian preaching would be expository preaching, that is, that all Christian instruction and exhortation would be drawn out of the passage which had been read."[3] Therefore, any kind of preaching as the week-by-week fare of pastoral proclamation other than exposition is a departure from the pattern of Christian ministry in the church.

One of the most overlooked facts about our heritage of exposition is that the chronology of the biblical Canon would suggest a gravitation toward exposition as the continuing approach to pastoral preaching. In building a case for a steady diet of contemporary narrative sermons, many people cite the *proportion* of narrative literature over against more didactic literature in the Bible. However, they often fail to consider the *order* in which the various genres fall. It appears that as God revealed His truth through the prophets and then in the Christ event, He utilized narrative literature extensively. But when it came time for that revelation to nurture the church on an ongoing basis through the apostles, He chose to use a host of epistles which obviously take on a more didactic and rhetorical form.

At the very least, the chronology of literary genres in Scripture suggests the possibility that narrative is much more conducive for revealing first-time stuff, while didactic is necessary for the explanation and application of the revelation. Even Calvin Miller, himself a strong proponent of narrative-style sermons, admitted that one weakness in a constant diet of narrative preaching is the loss of *didache,* or teaching, in the church. He said that "pressing the truths of the church may mean the sermon will have to answer the issue of Christian content on a more taxing level not entirely possible with the narrative sermon alone."[4]

The genes of exposition tragically lay almost completely dormant for almost a century and a half after the apostolic age with just a few exceptions. Some expository qualities were woven into some of the homilies of the patristic period (100–476 A.D.). While expositors were scarce during this time, a few faithful men carried the torch. The most significant expositor of the early Christian church was John Chrysostom, a leader of the Antiochene school. He rejected the common allegorical approach to interpretation and emphasized grammar and history in eloquent verse-by-verse and word-by-word expositions on many Bible books.

Although the Medieval period (476–1500) could easily be called a famine of exposition in history, a few gifted men did arise to counter the influence of scholastic theology and Aristotelian logic in biblical interpretation. Pre-Reformers like John Wyclif and William Tyndale denounced the preaching of their days and called for the rejection of sermons that did not treat the Scripture and interpret it literally. Others, like John Huss and Girolamo Savonarola, also were known as credible students and preachers of the Bible.

But the hereditary nature would once again raise its noble head at critical points in the history of the church. No reemergence was more pivotal than the revival of biblical exposition that arose in response to the glaring abuses of the indulgence system in Germany at the beginning of the sixteenth century. Without a doubt expository sermons were a primary vehicle for the prophetic voices which directly ignited the period of the Protestant Reformation (1500–1648 A.D.).

The sixteenth century was a great period for preaching in just about all areas. Preaching was restored to the central place in worship, new emphasis was placed on preparing men to preach, and the event as a whole gained a new respect. Preachers dealt plainly with problems and excesses regardless of the consequences. But probably the most significant quality was the revival of biblical preaching in which expository sermons driven by Scripture replaced the mere telling of stories of saints, martyrs, and miracles. These sermons were characterized by the employment of better methods of interpretation and application, a combination which fostered a much-needed revival of biblical preaching.

The list of great reformation expositors, of course, is headed by Martin Luther. After being appointed as professor at the University of Wittenberg in 1510, the Augustinian monk traveled to Rome the following year where he witnessed widespread corruption and worldliness among the clergy. Convinced of the need for reform, he returned to Wittenberg and began lecturing on the Psalms, Romans, Galatians, and Hebrews. After his conversion, Luther's opposition to the abuses of the indulgence practices prompted him to post his historic ninety-five theses on the church door at Wittenberg on October 31, 1517. The reformation proper had begun, and there is no doubt that expository sermons ushered it in and laid the foundation for the Protestant tradition.

Luther was joined by other reformers who approached their pulpits with firm convictions about biblical exposition in preaching. In 1519 in Zurich, Huldreich Ulrich Zwingli began to preach expositorily through the Book of Matthew and, in effect, the Swiss Reformation began. John Calvin wrote his famous *Institutes of Christianity* in 1536, firmly establishing him as one of the leading reformers. His sermons also were expository, logical in analysis, clear and unadorned, and intense and vigorous. Even though his exile interrupted an expositional series through the Book of Acts, he returned to his pulpit three years later and picked up with the very next verse where he had stopped! His commitment to exposition, earnest presentation, love of the truth, and devotion to duty made him one of the greatest preacher-theologians of all time. His incredible treatment of one Bible book after another in sequential expositions is unparalleled in church history.

The expository sermon continued to be a vital player in the church's life at numerous critical junctures. During the sixteenth and seventeenth centuries, the Puritans made the Bible central in Christian worship and championed for true preaching to be defined as the exposition of the Word of God. The polemic expositions of the "classic age" of the seventeenth-century British pulpit and the expository legacies of the Westminster pulpit under Morgan and Lloyd-Jones could be explored as additional seasons when the recessive genes of exposition surfaced. But the alternative forms of pastoral preaching which contributed to the spiritual condition that necessitated the reformation are enough to tell us that the approach that fostered and nurtured the resurgence is what is needed for healthy congregations today.

Pastors and congregations can be certain that exposition is hereditary in pastoral preaching. Regarding biblical truth, we have been given the responsibility to explain it, not reveal it. And the only authority we have to do so is wrapped up in its divine origin, finality, and completeness. There is nothing we can do about it, even if we wanted to. To attempt to do so is to deny the very nature of preaching itself, not to mention the faithfulness of our forefathers throughout history. The connection that pastors today have with the responsibility to expose God's voice in our sermons is a condition about which we have no choice. It ties us to both our forefathers and our heavenly Father. And through it we follow them and exalt Him. While it may have been recessive in some generations, it's still in the genes!

Deliver to Your Descendants

At the 1988 summer Olympics in Seoul, Korea, the U.S. team was highly favored to win the sprint relay. Carl Lewis, considered the fastest man in the world at the time, was supposed to run the anchor leg. But the U.S. team was so loaded with talent that the coach decided to run some other sprinters in the preliminaries and save the A team for the finals. The U.S. never got to run in the finals. In one of the preliminary races, Calvin Smith and Lee McNeil made the exchange of the baton illegally between the third and fourth leg. Smith apparently was unsteady with the handoff, and McNeil failed to provide a stable target. The team was disqualified. Why? Because in a relay race, the exchange of the baton has to take place within a limited area, and the U.S. team was outside the allowed zone! The baton has to be exchanged within a particular area in order for the exchange to be valid.

What a tragedy—to lose a race, not because you do not have the fastest runners or the best team, and not even because you drop the baton. But you lose because you fail to make the exchange of the baton within the required zone. Our generation is the only zone we have been given in which to make the exchange. Success for us is not determined by how fast we run, how big our churches are, or how grand our numbers. Success is determined by our faithfulness to deliver the baton within our zone so our descendants can take it from here. Dear pastor and people, time is running out! We must make a steady handoff and provide a stable target. So deliver the faith with which you have been entrusted to your spiritual descendants before it's too late!

Where Do I Go from Here . . .

Biblical exposition is the only sure way for the pastor to equip the modern church to hand off the heritage of the Christian faith to the next generation. People can listen to topical how-to and life application sermons all their lives and never really get a grasp on general Bible knowledge, Christian doctrine, or systematic and biblical theology. Only as the Word of God is systematically and intentionally explained and applied do believers "come to the unity of the faith and of the knowledge of the Son of God, to a perfect man, to the measure of the stature of the fullness of Christ" (Eph. 4:13). Then and only then will they be able to "commit these to faithful men who will be able to teach others also" (2 Tim. 2:2).

Beloved Christian, help your pastor to expound God's Word by encouraging him, praying for him, and ministering with him so that he may give adequate attention to exposing the truth in every text. And dear pastor, preach the Bible for God's glory so that your people become a faith community that knows Christian doctrine well enough to pass it along to the next runners!

Summation

I still have some questions.

I wonder why so many pastors submit themselves to the pressure of trying to answer all the questions people are asking today. I'm curious why so many teaching shepherds are spending their time trying to be experts in so many fields, to the neglect of the primary field to which God called them. I'd really like to know how the pastors who are making such attempts ever find time to study the Bible to actually find out what God says. I wonder why so many pastors are playing Russian Roulette with the needs of their people by offering quick fix-it sermons instead of equipping them with the ongoing source of wisdom and knowledge through the indwelling Christ.

I'm also curious as to why so many people who listen to sermons place unrealistic demands on their pastors by expecting them to be all-knowing gurus. I'd like to know why so many believers continue to expose themselves and their families to the fluff of *good stuff* that flows from so many pulpits. I wonder why so many people would rather gamble on getting just the right sermon this Sunday for their particular need as opposed to simply welcoming another opportunity to have their spirits nurtured so they have the mind of Christ for every circumstance.

In this book I have made absolutely no attempt to delineate a homiletic that addresses the intricacies of sermon making and delivery. I've not tried to deal with the varieties of sermon introductions, outlines, developments, or conclusions. This work has not concerned itself with the interesting subjects of illustrations, titles, or even mediums of delivery. These and other topics of discussion certainly have their place in the study of the art of preaching. But they are lesser matters when compared to the lofty nature of preaching itself.

This book, instead, has been a humble attempt to extract a practical theology of pastoral preaching from the Bible. Its foundational premise is that preaching—and the sermons that express it—must be driven by a passion for the glory of God. Admittedly, it's a narrow perspective that goes against the grain of much preaching practice today. But narrow is not always bad. Regarding coming to Him, our Lord said that we should "enter by the narrow gate; for wide is the gate and broad is the way that leads to destruction, and there are many who go in by it. Because narrow is the gate and difficult is the way which leads to life, and there are few who find it" (Matt. 7:13–14). While this practical theology by no means claims to be the way to eternal life, my prayer is that it may be the narrow gate by which some pastors and congregants find new life in the sermon event. Truly it's a narrow gate, and the way may be difficult at first. But the end of the road is glorious!

I've struggled in my attempt to address both those who preach and those who listen to preaching in the local church. Forgive me where my efforts were confusing. But I am firmly convinced that the fruit of the approach to preaching posited in this book will only fully be realized when both preacher and people are on the same page. So, if you are a pastor who embraces this narrow way, I challenge you to get this book in the hands of as many of the people who listen to you preach as possible. If you are a noble listener of sermons in a local church and long to be fed with *God's stuff* as opposed to mere *good stuff*, leave a copy of the book on your pastor's desk. If he's an expositor, it will encourage him. If he's not, I pray it will beckon him to enter the narrow gate.

Now go preach and listen to preaching for the glory of God!

Endnotes

Foreword

1. D. Martyn Lloyd-Jones, *Preaching and Preachers* (Grand Rapids: Zondervan, 1971), 14–15.

Chapter 1

1. Paul himself equated the teaching of the Old Testament with the Christ event he confessed here in the Corinthian text. See Acts 13:13–41; 17:2–3; 28:23.

2. Leon Morris, *The First Epistle of Paul to the Corinthians*, in Tyndale New Testament Commentaries (Grand Rapids: Eerdmans, 1958), 46.

3. James W. Thompson, *Preaching like Paul: Homiletical Wisdom for Today* (Louisville: Westminster John Knox, 2001), 48.

4. Jill Morgan, A Man of the Word (Grand Rapids: Baker, 1972), 39–40.

5. Jerry Vines and Jim Shaddix, *Power in the Pulpit* (Chicago: Moody, 1999), 55.

6. Billy Graham, *Just As I Am: The Autobiography of Billy Graham* (New York: Zondervan, 1997), 138–39.

Chapter 2

1. "Short Takes," *Time*, 7 December 1992, 83.

2. F. W. Grosheide, *Commentary on the First Epistle to the Corinthians*, in The New International Commentary on the New Testament (Grand Rapids: Wm. B. Eerdmans, 1953), 58.

3. Charles Colson and Nancy Pearcey, *How Now Shall We Live?* (Wheaton: Tyndale House, 1999), 471.

4. Norman Rose, *Churchill: The Unruly Giant* (New York, NY: The Free Press, 1994), 55.

5. Ibid., 56.

6. H. A. Ironside, *Addresses on the First Epistle to the Corinthians* (New York: Loizeaux Brothers, 1938), 87.

7. John Piper, *The Supremacy of God in Preaching* (Grand Rapids: Baker, 1990), 33.

8. Ibid., 35.

9. Ironside, *Addresses*, 87.

10. John Knox, *The Integrity of Preaching* (Nashville: Abingdon, 1957), 89.

Chapter 3

1. R. C. H. Lenski, *The Interpretation of St. Paul's First and Second Epistles to the Corinthians* (Minneapolis: Augsburg, 1937), 94.

2. See Thompson, *Preaching like Paul*, 85. He identifies two changes that have diminished the pastoral dimension of the sermon: (1) the development of multistaff churches, making pastoral care a specialized ministry, and (2) the recent emphasis on narrative preaching, causing the sermon to speak by indirection rather than confronting listeners with the call for changed lives.

3. Thomas Long, *The Witness of Preaching* (Louisville: Westminster/ John Knox, 1989), 33.

4. Ronald Allen, "The Relationship between the Pastoral and the Prophetic in Preaching," *Encounter* 49 (1988): 174.

5. Harry Emerson Fosdick, "What Is the Matter with Preaching?" *Harper's* 107 (July 1928): 134.

6. Gary D. Stratman, *Pastoral Preaching* (Nashville: Abingdon, 1983), 9.

7. Thompson, *Preaching like Paul*, 87–88.

8. See Grosheide, *Commentary*, 41.

9. Lenski, *Interpretation*, 52.

Part 2

1. Charles Jefferson, *The Minister as Shepherd* (Hong Kong: Living Books for All, 1980), 59, 61.

2. See John MacArthur Jr., "What Is a Pastor to Be and Do?" in *Rediscovering Pastoral Ministry*, ed. John MacArthur Jr. (Dallas: Word, 1995), 28. The pastoral epistles especially are filled with exhortations to provide the flock with spiritual nourishment and to protect them from heresy, all via the instruction of right doctrine (see 1 Tim. 1:3–4; 3:1; 4:6–7, 13–16; 5:17–18; 6:1–5, 20–21; 2 Tim. 1:6–8, 13–14; 2:1–2, 8–9, 14–16; 3:14–17; 4:1–5; Titus 1:7–14; 2:1, 15).

Chapter 4

1. Walter Kaiser, "The Crisis in Expository Preaching," *Preaching*, September/October 1995, 6.

2. Jerry Vines and Jim Shaddix, *Power in the Pulpit* (Chicago: Moody Press, 1999), (58–59).

3. Four other references to a "tree of life" do exist in the Bible outside of Genesis and Revelation, but they appear to be metaphorical as opposed to literal. See Proverbs 3:18; 11:30; 13:12; 15:4. The use of the definite article in the Genesis and Revelation references and the absence of it in the Proverbs references also support this distinction.

4. James F. Stitzinger, "The History of Expository Preaching," in John MacArthur Jr., *Rediscovering Expository Preaching*, ed. Richard L. Mayhue (Dallas: Word, 1992), 38–42.

5. Bill Hull, *Right Thinking* (Colorado Springs: Navpress, 1985), 8.

Chapter 5

1. Lester Thonssen, ed., *Selected Readings in Rhetoric and Public Speaking* (New York: Wilson Press, 1942), 36.

2. Charles S. Kelley Jr., *How Did They Do It? The Story of Southern Baptist Evangelism* (New Orleans: Insight Press, 1993), 59.

3. Thompson, *Selected Readings,* 75.

4. Ibid., 83–84.

5. Ibid., 76. Thompson bases his contentions on a very strong case for a similarity between Paul's preaching and writing styles. See Thompson, 75–84.

6. George Kennedy, *New Testament Interpretation through Rhetorical Criticism* (Chapel Hill: University of North Carolina Press, 1984), 86–87.

7. Ibid.

8. As quoted in John F. MacArthur Jr., *1 Corinthians,* in The MacArthur New Testament Commentary, (Chicago: Moody Press, 1983), 57.

9. John MacArthur Jr., *2 Timothy,* in The MacArthur New Testament Commentaries (Chicago: Moody Press, 1995), 163.

10. John MacArthur Jr., *Romans 1–8,* in The MacArthur New Testament Commentary (Chicago: Moody Press, 1991), 491–92.

Chapter 6

1. Haddon Robinson, "The Heresy of Application," *Leadership,* Fall 1997, 20.

2. Piper, *Supremacy of God,* 10.

3. A. W. Tozer, *Of God and Men* (Harrisburg, Pa.: Christian Publications, 1960), 26–27.

4. Haddon W. Robinson, *Biblical Preaching,* 2nd ed. (Grand Rapids: Baker, 2001), 108.

5. See H. C. Brown Jr., H. Gordon Clinard, and Jesse J. Northcutt, *Steps to the Sermon* (Nashville: Broadman, 1963), 16–17; Al Fasol, *Essentials for Biblical Preaching* (Grand Rapids: Baker, 1989), 57; Robinson, *Biblical Preaching,* 109–10; Vines and Shaddix, 139.

6. Thompson, *Selected Readings,* 83.

7. Francis A. Schaeffer, *How Should We Then Live?* (Wheaton: Crossway Books, 1976), 19.

8. J. Daniel Baumann, *An Introduction to Contemporary Preaching* (Grand Rapids: Baker, 1972), 13.

9. See Thompson, *Selected Readings,* 93–94, regarding Paul's apparent intentionality about establishing the identity of his communities.

10. Thompson, 98–99.

11. Richard Hays, *The Moral Vision of the New Testament* (San Francisco: Harper/San Francisco, 1996), 197.

Chapter 7

1. John A. Broadus, *On the Preparation and Delivery of Sermons,* 4th ed., revised by Vernon L. Stanfield (San Francisco: Harper and Row Publishers, 1979), 19.

2. H. C. Brown Jr., *A Quest for Reformation in Preaching* (Nashville: Broadman Press, 1968), 88.

3. Joseph M. Stowell, *Shepherding the Church into the 21st Century* (Wheaton: Victor, 1994), 223.

4. Kaiser, "The Crisis," 6.

5. MacArthur, *1 Corinthians*, 55.

6. F. F. Bruce, *I and II Corinthians*, The New Century Bible Commentary, eds. Ronald E. Clements and Matthew Black (London: Marshall, Morgan, and Scott, 1971), 133.

7. Grosheide, *Commentary*, 333.

8. MacArthur, *1 Corinthians*, 384.

Chapter 8

1. Kenneth L. Woodward, "In the Beginning, There Were the Holy Books," *Newsweek*, 11 February 2002, 54.

2. Bryan Chapell, *Christ-Centered Preaching: Redeeming the Expository Sermon* (Grand Rapids: Baker Book House, 1994), 24.

3. Stowell, *Shepherding the Church*, 223.

4. Donald Miller, *The Way to Biblical Preaching* (New York: Abingdon Press, 1957), 26.

5. See Brown, *Quest for Reformation*, 71–133, and Al Fasol, *Essentials for Biblical Preaching* (Grand Rapids: Baker, 1989), 89–96.

6. Brown, *Quest for Reformation*, 105.

7. Ibid.

8. John R. W. Stott, *Guard the Truth* (Downers Grove, Ill.: InterVarsity Press, 1996), 22.

9. Richard C. White, *Biblical Preaching* (St. Louis: CBP Press, 1988), 19.

10. E. M. Bounds, *Power Through Prayer* (London: Marshall, Morgan and Scott, n.d.; reprint, Grand Rapids: Baker, 1991), 69 (page citations are to the reprint edition).

11. Ibid., 76.

12. White, *Biblical Preaching*, 20. White rightly concludes that the reason the preacher adopts this approach is "because that's the way he or she has always gone about doing topical sermons (the way the preacher was taught and sees colleagues doing it), and hasn't been taught that certain such activities should be set aside and replaced when doing biblical sermons."

Chapter 9

1. Calvin Miller, "Narrative Preaching," in *Handbook of Contemporary Preaching*, ed. by Michael Duduit (Nashville: Broadman & Holman, 1992), 108.

2. Elizabeth Achtemeier, *Preaching as Theology & Art* (Nashville: Abingdon Press, 1984), 17.

3. Stott, *Guard the Truth*, 22.

4. Miller, "Narrative Preaching," 111. See Miller, 104–112, for a good assessment of the strengths, weaknesses, and goals of narrative preaching.